Scott, Foresman

English That Works 2

ICB-VESL
Integrated, Competency-based, Bilingual, pre-Vocational English as a Second Language

Authors
K. Lynn Savage
Mamie How
Ellen Lai-shan Yeung

Project Director
David Hemphill

Project Sponsor
Chinatown Resources Development Center
San Francisco, California

Scott, Foresman and Company
Lifelong Learning Division
Glenview, IL • Dallas, TX • Oakland, NJ • Palo Alto, CA • Tucker, GA

ISBN: 0-673-24552-7

Adapted with the aid and participation
of the Chinatown Resources
Development Center from the program
developed by the Center and published
as *Integrated Competency-Based
Bilingual Vocational English as a
Second Language.* Copyright © 1980
Chinatown Resources Development
Center.
This work was developed under a state-
administered grant of federal funds
(P.L. 91-230, Section 310) from the
California State Department of
Education, 721 Capitol Mall,
Sacramento, CA 95814. However, the
content does not necessarily reflect the
position or policy of the Department or
of the U.S. Department of Health,
Education and Welfare; and no official
endorsement of this work should be
inferred.

Table of Contents

About This Book

This book is part of a comprehensive program for adults who want to learn English that will help them get and keep a job. The program includes two student books, each of which has a detailed *Teacher's Edition*, as well as flash cards, cassettes, and *Cultural Notes* booklets. The final goal of each of the five units in this book is the completion of one real-life task. Each unit has six instructional lessons and one review lesson.

The first part of each instructional lesson develops language; the second part develops skills for getting or keeping a job. The language half of each lesson includes the sections called **Getting Ready, Conversation, Exercises,** and **Write a Story** or **Read a Story.** The **Getting Ready** drills introduce language items that will appear in the conversation. The drills are usually two-line exchanges in with underlined words or phrases that can be replaced with other vocabulary items that are presented visually. Flashcards of these items cue responses for additional practice. The **Conversation** section develops listening skills and provides extensive individual oral practice. When books are closed and the tape is played, the **Conversation** encourages development of listening-comprehension skills. When books are open and students work in pairs, it develops oral fluency. Each student takes the role of one of the speakers, replacing the underlined words with the visual vocabulary items. The students then alternate roles. The **Exercises** section provides additional practice with the grammatical focus of the conversation. Some exercises call for written answers to questions. Others do not provide writing space, but rather are flexibly designed so that pairs of students can practice questions and answers orally or so that individuals can practice writing the structure of the question, the answer, or both. The final section in the language half of each lesson is either **Write a Story** or **Read a Story.** The purpose of the **Write a Story** section is to develop composition skills. Students first fill in the missing words in a cloze paragraph, and then, using the cloze as a model, they compose an original paragraph based on their own experience. The purpose of the **Read a Story** section is to present in prose style the vocabulary and structures already practiced orally. The prose passages focus on situations with which students can readily identify and on topics that will stimulate class discussion.

The second half of each instructional lesson applies the language to a specific communication or problem-solving skill. It includes the **Tasks** and **On Your Own** sections, and frequently begins with another **Getting Ready.** This **Getting Ready** introduces language necessary for recognition, but not required for production. It may include a presentation of concepts essential for mastery of a skill. **Tasks** then presents a hypothetical situation, and students must use that skill to solve a problem. The teacher may use the **Tasks** as a class activity, guiding the students through the steps, or as an individual activity that develops student initiative, independence, and skill in following directions. **On Your Own** requires students to apply the language and skills learned to their own situations and communities. When local resources such as maps are required or recommended, these are listed in the front section of the *Teacher's Edition*.

The review lesson at the end of each unit integrates the content and skills of the preceding lessons and checks student mastery of specific language items. The lesson opens with an extended conversation that combines the conversations from all previous lessons in the unit. In the **Check Your Listening** section, two exercises provide directed listening activities for the extended conversation. In the **Conversation Review** section, a partially completed conversation provides the framework for students to practice in pairs, using information from their personal experience. **Check Your Vocabulary** and **Check Your Grammar** test student mastery of specific language items. The **Read and Think** section summarizes concepts presented in the unit, presents questions to check comprehension, and poses problems for students to solve. The final section, **Put It Together,** integrates the skills items from the various lessons. Students may apply these skills to a given hypothetical situation or to themselves and their community.

The *Cultural Notes* booklet that accompanies the student book is available in several languages. This supplement presents the objectives and the importance of the objectives for each unit, and a list of vocabulary words and their translations for each lesson. It also provides cultural notes for each lesson in cases of items that cannot be easily translated. An English version of all the material in the native language component appears in the front section of the *Teacher's Edition*.

Unit 1
Job Experience

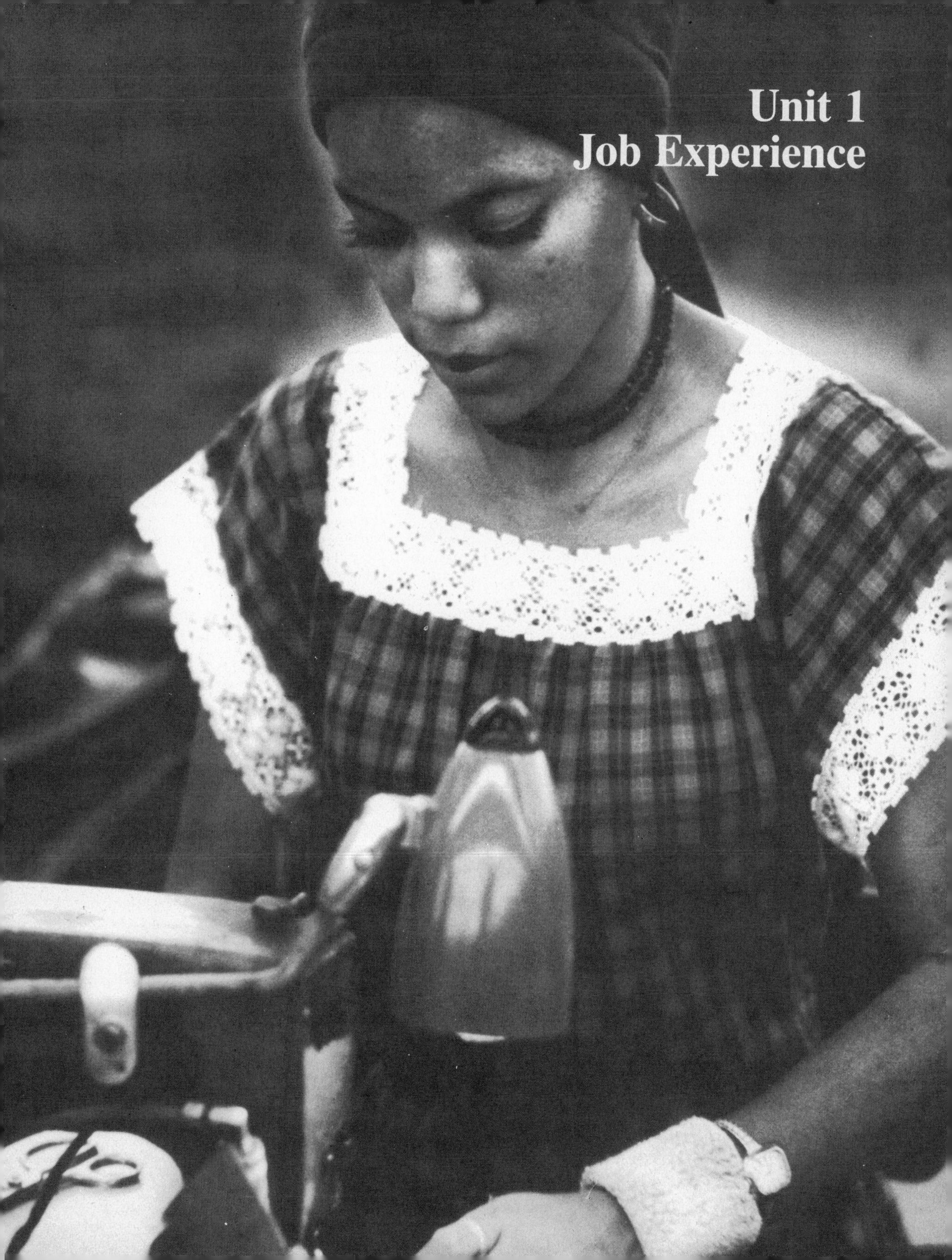

Lesson One/1

Getting Ready

1. *How long* were you <u>a sales clerk</u>?
   I was <u>a sales clerk</u> *for* ten years.

2. He *was* <u>a sales clerk</u> and she *was too*. BUT
   He *wasn't* <u>a sales clerk</u> and she *wasn't either*.

Conversation

Applicant 1: Are you working now?
Applicant 2: No, I'm not. Are you?
Applicant 1: No, I'm not either.
Applicant 2: What was your last job?
Applicant 1: I was <u>a sales clerk</u>.
What about you?
Applicant 2: I was <u>a sales clerk</u> too.
Applicant 1: Really? (For) how long?

Applicant 2: (For) ten years. And you?
Applicant 1: (For) five years.
Applicant 2: Well, I hope you find a job soon.
Applicant 1: Thank you. I hope you do too.

1. sales clerk

2. electrician

3. receptionist

4. hair stylist

5. stock clerk

6. welder

Exercises

A. Finish the sentences with "too" or "either."

1. I'm not working, and he isn't working _____.

2. He was a sales clerk, and she was a sales clerk _____.

3. I worked for ten years, and he worked for ten years _____.

4. She doesn't have a job now, and he doesn't have a job now _____.

5. James didn't work last month, and Ira didn't work last month _____.

6. I'm looking for a job, and my brother is looking for a job _____.

B. Write a question and then write the answer. Follow the model.

[Cindy Jansen]
[six months]

1. *How long was Cindy Jansen a welder? She was a welder for six months.*

[Peter Grant]
[five years]

2. _____
_____
_____
_____

[Irene Williams]
[two months]

3. _____
_____
_____
_____

Write a Story

A. Read the paragraph and then write one word in each blank.

George _____ from the Soviet Union. _____ sister is from the Soviet
       (1)   (2)

Union _____. George _____ an electrician _____ eight years.
       (3)   (4)   (5)

_____ sister was _____ receptionist for four years. George _____ married
  (6)   (7)   (8)

and his sister is married _____.
                            (9)

B. Write a story about yourself and someone in your family on a separate piece of
paper. Use the paragraph above as a model.

Getting Ready

1. When you write dates on an application form, you can use abbreviations for most
of the months.

January = Jan.	May	September = Sept.
February = Feb.	June	October = Oct.
March = Mar.	July	November = Nov.
April = Apr.	August = Aug.	December = Dec.

2. There are two ways to order work experience on an application form:

FIRST JOB FIRST (chronological order)	LAST JOB FIRST (reverse chronological order)
January 15, 1969	March 27, 1973
December 1, 1969	December 1, 1969
March 27, 1973	January 15, 1969

Now order these dates:

	CHRONOLOGICAL ORDER	REVERSE CHRONOLOGICAL ORDER
December 6, 1972	_____	_____
January 29, 1969	_____	_____
May 17, 1974	_____	_____
April 18, 1965	_____	_____

3. Application forms often have boxes for dates. Sometimes the boxes are big, but sometimes they are small.

In a big box write the short form of the month:

> DATES EMPLOYED
> From *Sept., 1975* To *Aug., 1979*

In a small box write a number for the month:

> DATES EMPLOYED   From   To
>   *9/75* *8/79*

4. When you still have a job, write "present"* under "To" for "Dates Employed."

Sam got a job as an electrician in 1979. He is still an electrician.

> DATES EMPLOYED   From   To
>   *1979*   *Present*

---

*present = now

Tasks

Read the stories and then complete the forms.

1. Joe was a carpenter from June, 1972, to February, 1974. He was a waiter from April, 1974, to September, 1976. He got a job as a cashier in September, 1976. He is still a cashier.

EMPLOYMENT RECORD (Begin with your present or last job.)		
JOB TITLE	DATES EMPLOYED From	To
JOB TITLE	DATES EMPLOYED From	To
JOB TITLE	DATES EMPLOYED From	To

2. Mary was a typist from April, 1968 to December, 1971. She was an accounting clerk from January, 1972 to May, 1974. Then she got a job as a bookkeeper in July, 1974. She is still a bookkeeper.

EMPLOYMENT RECORD (Begin with your first job.)		
NAME OF POSITION	DATES WORKED From	To
NAME OF POSITION	DATES WORKED From	To
NAME OF POSITION	DATES WORKED From	To

On Your Own

Complete the forms for yourself.

EMPLOYMENT RECORD Begin with your first job.		
NAME OF POSITION	DATES WORKED From	To
NAME OF POSITION	DATES WORKED From	To
NAME OF POSITION	DATES WORKED From	To

EMPLOYMENT RECORD Begin with your present or last job.	
NAME OF POSITION	DATES EMPLOYED From To
NAME OF POSITION	DATES EMPLOYED From To
NAME OF POSITION	DATES EMPLOYED From To

Lesson Two/2

Getting Ready

1. Where did you work?
   I worked *in* a <u>department store</u>. (in a laundry, in a school, . . .)   BUT
   I worked *on* a farm.

2. What did you do?
   I <u>recorded sales</u>.

3.
<u>counted supplies</u>	1975–76
<u>recorded sales</u>	1977–78

   What did you do *after* you <u>counted supplies</u>?
   I <u>recorded sales</u>.
   What did you do *before* you <u>recorded sales</u>?
   I <u>counted supplies</u>.

Conversation

Interviewer: What kind of work experience do you have?
Applicant: In <u>*(student's country)*</u> I worked <u>in</u> a <u>department store</u>
for several years.
Interviewer: What did you do?
Applicant: I <u>recorded sales</u>.
Interviewer: What did you do before that?
Applicant: I <u>counted supplies</u> (before that).
Interviewer: Do you have local experience?
Applicant: No, I'm afraid I don't. But I learn fast.

record sales
1. [department store]

count supplies

mend clothes
2. [laundry]

sort laundry

grade papers | duplicate lessons | sand wood | paint furniture
3. [school] | | **4.** [carpenter shop]

load trucks | crate vegetables | tend bar | wait on tables
5. [farm] | | **6.** [restaurant]

Exercises

Look at the pictures and the words. Make questions and then answer them. Follow the model.

QUESTION	ANSWER
What did Bob do after he counted supplies?	*He recorded sales after he counted supplies.*
What did Bob do before he recorded sales?	*He counted supplies before he recorded sales.*

[Bob]  [Andy]

1. ['74–'77] ['77–'78]   **2.** [1:00–3:00 p.m.] [3:00–5:00 p.m.]

[Blanca]

3. ['79–'80] ['78–'79]

[Victor]

5. ['76–'78] ['78–'80]

[Beth]

4. [Sunday] [Monday]

Write a Story

A. Read the paragraph. Then write one word in each blank.

Ming-po is _____ Taiwan. _____ Taiwan _____ worked _____
      (1)   (2)   (3)   (4)

a school _____ one year. _____ graded papers _____ six months.
         (5)   (6)   (7)

_____ that she duplicated lessons _____ six months. She has
(8)   (9)

_____ local experience.
(10)

B. Write a story about yourself on a separate piece of paper. Use the paragraph above as a model.

Getting Ready

Application forms ask for information about job duties.

a. For past jobs use past time.

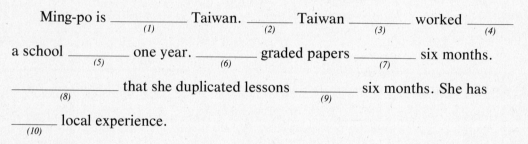

TITLE	EMPLOYED		DUTIES
	From	To	
clerk	4/68	12/71	sorted mail, filed, typed letters

b. For present jobs use present time.

TITLE	EMPLOYED		DUTIES
	From	To	
clerk	*7/78*	*present*	*sort mail, file, type letters*

Tasks

A. Read the story and complete the form.

     Misha Varig is a stock clerk now. He counts supplies, moves boxes, and stocks shelves. He got the job in June, 1980. Before that he was a mail clerk. He wrapped and weighed packages and loaded trucks. He worked as a mail clerk from June, 1979, to May, 1980. Before he was a mail clerk, he was a service station attendant. He pumped gas, washed windows, changed oil, and changed tires. He was a service station attendant from May, 1978, to June, 1979.

APPLICANT'S NAME:		
EMPLOYMENT RECORD (Begin with your first job.)		
POSITION	FROM/TO	DUTIES

B. Find a classmate. One looks at the form, asks questions, listens to the answers, and writes. One listens to the questions, reads the story, and answers the questions.

ASK	ANSWER
What is Bennett's job now?	*He's a bartender.*
When did he begin?	*in . . .*
What are his duties?	
What did he do before that? . . .	

Bennett Lee is a bartender now. He got the job in February, 1979. He takes orders, mixes drinks, washes glasses, and collects money. Before he was a bartender he was a waiter. He waited on tables, took orders, and cleaned tables. He was a waiter from January, 1978, to January, 1979. Before that he was a kitchen helper. He washed dishes and washed and peeled vegetables. He was a kitchen helper for six months, from July to December, 1978.

APPLICANT'S NAME: _____			
	last	first	middle

EMPLOYMENT RECORD Begin with your present or last job first.

JOB TITLE	DATES EMPLOYED		DUTIES
	From	To	

On Your Own

A. Complete the form for yourself.

EMPLOYMENT RECORD (Please list jobs in chronological order.)			
JOB TITLE	DATES EMPLOYED		JOB DUTIES
	From	To	

B. Find a classmate. Ask questions, listen to the answers, and complete the form.

NAME OF APPLICANT _____
(last)   (first)   (middle)   (maiden)

EMPLOYMENT RECORD Please list jobs in reverse chronological order (present or most recent job first).		
JOB TITLE	FROM/TO	JOB DUTIES

Lesson Three/3

Getting Ready

1. What kind of experience do you have?
   I have experience *as* a <u>mail clerk</u>.

2. What kind of equipment did you use?
   I used equipment like <u>hand trucks</u>.

3. What kind of tools did you use?
   I used tools like <u>electric drills</u>.

Conversation

Interviewer: I understand you have several years of local experience.

Applicant: That's right. (I have) three years (experience) as <u>a mail clerk</u>.

Interviewer: What kind of <u>equipment</u> did you use?

Applicant: (I used) <u>equipment</u> like <u>hand trucks</u>, <u>postage meters</u>, . . .

Interviewer: Good. We can use someone with your skills.

EQUIPMENT   TOOLS

hand truck   postage meter   electric drill   power saw
1. [mail clerk]   **2.** [carpenter]

EQUIPMENT   TOOLS

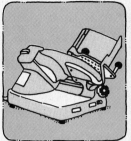

slicer   grinder   sander   spray gun
3. [butcher]   **4.** [painter]

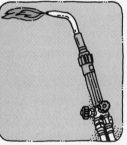

tractor   fork lift   blow torch   impact wrench
5. [farm worker]   **6.** [auto mechanic]

Exercises

A. Look at the pictures and the words. Make a question and then answer it using
"like." Follow the models.

QUESTION	ANSWER
What kind of equipment does a mail clerk use?	*A mail clerk uses equipment like postage meters and hand trucks.*
What kind of things does a laundry worker do?	*A laundry worker does things like sort and mend clothes.*

1. [equipment/mail clerk]   **2.** [things/laundry worker]

3. [equipment/farm worker]

4. [tools/carpenter]

5. [things/farm worker]

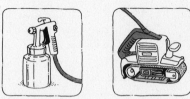

6. [tools/painter]

B. Read the question and then write the answer.

1. What kind of tools do you use? _____

_____

2. What kind of equipment do you use? _____

_____

3. What kind of things can you do? _____

_____

Write a Story

A. Read the paragraph and then write one word in each blank.

Carmen Galante just came _____ this country. She has no _____

(1)   (2)

experience, but she has eight years _____ experience as a farm worker _____

(3)   (4)

Cuba. She used equipment like tractors and _____ lifts. Before

(5)

_____ she was a mail _____ for two years. She used
(6)   (7)

_____ like hand trucks and postage _____.
(8)   (9)

B. Write a story about yourself. Use the paragraph above as a model.

_____

_____

_____

_____

_____

_____

_____

_____

_____

Getting Ready

Application forms ask for information about tools or equipment. Don't write things like "scissors" because you don't have to learn how to use them.

JOB TITLE: *Mail clerk*	Equipment or tools used:
JOB DUTIES: *Sorted Mail, Weighed Packages*	*Postage Meter* *Adding Machine* *~~Scissors~~*

Tasks

Read the stories and complete the forms.

1.   Linda Gomez is looking for a job. Her last job was in a school. She was a mail clerk. She mailed letters and packages. She used a hand truck, a postage meter, and a photocopier.

Job title: _____   Equipment or tools used:

_____

Job duties: _____

_____

_____

_____

2.   Anwar Tahari is looking for a job. His last job was in a furniture store. He was a carpenter. He made shelves and furniture. He used power tools like electric drills and power saws.

Position you occupied—what were your duties?

_____

_____

Did you operate any equipment?

_____

_____

On Your Own

Complete the form for yourself.

List jobs you have held (begin with your last job):		
Exact title	Describe what you did	Equipment or tools used
Exact title	Describe what you did	Equipment or tools used
Exact title	Describe what you did	Equipment or tools used

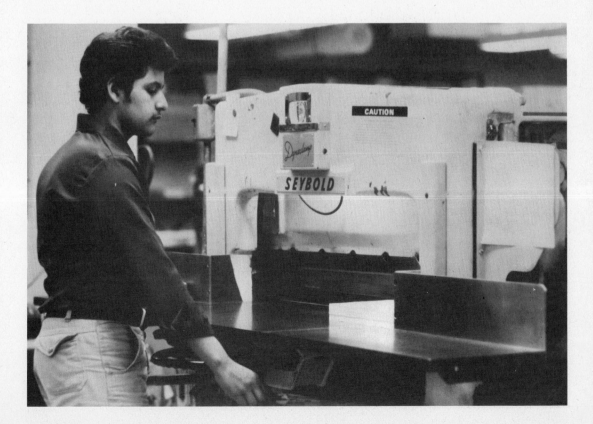

Lesson Four/4

Getting Ready

1. *Why* did you leave your last job?
   I left *because* <u>my mother was ill.</u>

2. I left my job because <u>my mother was ill.</u>
   You should write "<u>family illness.</u>"

Conversation

Maria: Do you have a minute? I need some advice.
Hugo: Sure. What kind of advice?
Maria: I left my last job because <u>my mother was ill</u>. What should I put down on my application form?
Hugo: I think you should write "<u>family illness.</u>"
Maria: <u>Family illness</u>? O.K. Thanks for the advice.

1. my mother was ill   family illness

2. my husband was ill   family illness

3. I hurt my back   injury

4. I hurt my neck   injury

5. I got married — family responsibility

6. I was pregnant — family responsibility

Exercises

Read the question, look at the picture, and then write the answer. Follow the model.

1. Why did Peg leave her last job? *She left her last job because she hurt her back.*

2. Why did Jill leave her job? _____

_____

3. Why did Ann leave her last job? _____

_____

4. Why did Pam leave her job? _____

_____

5. Why did Rita leave her job? _____

_____

6. Why did Jan leave her job? _____

_____

Read a Story

Read the story and then answer the questions.

Companies want information about the former employers of job applicants. They want information about both the company and the supervisor because they want to check the information applicants give them. When you give this information, write complete names and addresses. For *Name of Company,* don't just put *restaurant*. Put the name of the restaurant too (for example, *Far East Restaurant*). For *Address of Company,* don't just put the name of the city. Put the address, state, and zip code too. For *Name of Supervisor,* don't just put *Mr. White*. Put his first name or his initials too (for example, *Mr. Joseph White* or *Mr. J. L. White*).

Questions

1. Why do employers want the complete name and address of companies and supervisors?
2. Is *restaurant* the name of a company?
3. For a complete address, what four things do you need?
4. Is *Mr. White* a complete name?
5. Do you have to put your supervisor's first name?

<u>What Do You Think?</u>

1. Elena Gonzalez worked in a restaurant in Mexico. She is applying for a job in Dallas now. Should she put the name of the restaurant on her application form?
2. Soon Park quit his last job because he didn't like the supervisor. Should he put the name of the supervisor on his application form?

Getting Ready

1. Application forms usually ask the reason for leaving a job. When you leave for a personal reason, write the general category. Don't write specific reasons. Most personal reasons are in one of three general categories: (a) family illness (b) injury   (c) family responsibilities

2. Another personal reason for leaving a job is because you move. When you move from one country to another, write *immigrated*.

Tasks

A. Read the specific reason for leaving, and then write the general category in the box.

REASON FOR LEAVING

1. I hurt my back.

2. My children were sick.

3. I got married.

4. My mother died.

5. I hurt my hand.

6. I came to the United States.

7. My husband was ill.

B. Read the stories and complete the forms.

1.   Eve Taylor is looking for a job. Her last employer was the Fast Taxi Company. The company's address is 4565 Mission Avenue, San Diego, California 92116. She was an accounting clerk and her supervisor was Sam Kean, the accounting manager.

NAME AND ADDRESS OF COMPANY	NAME OF SUPERVISOR
	TITLE OF SUPERVISOR

2.   Bill Flynn is looking for a job. His last employer was the Century Furniture
Company. The company's address was 410 Park Avenue, New York, N.Y.
10022. His job was making furniture. His supervisor was John Bayer, the
foreman.

NAME OF COMPANY	SUPERVISOR: NAME
ADDRESS	TITLE

On Your Own

Complete the form for yourself.

EMPLOYMENT RECORD Begin with your present or last job.	
Name of Company	Address
Supervisor: Name and Title	
Name of Company	Address
Supervisor: Name and Title	
Name of Company	Address
Supervisor: Name and Title	

Lesson Five/5

Getting Ready

1. Why do you want to quit?
   The <u>work</u> <u>is</u> too <u>dangerous</u>
   for me.

2. What kind of job are you looking for?
   I'm looking for a job with good
   <u>working conditions</u>.

Conversation

Charlie: Are you still working at the same place?
Sandra: Yes, but I want to quit.
Charlie: Why?
Sandra: The <u>work</u> <u>is</u> too <u>dangerous</u> for me.
Charlie: Is that the only reason?
Sandra: No (it isn't). There are also other problems.
Charlie: Then what are you going to do?
Sandra: (I'm going to) look for a job with better <u>working conditions</u>.

WORKING CONDITIONS:

1. work/dangerous

2. job/boring

3. hours/long

BENEFITS:

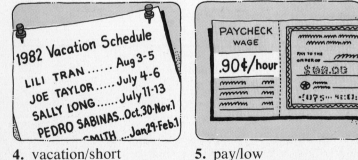

4. vacation/short   **5.** pay/low   **6.** health plan/limited

OPPORTUNITIES:

  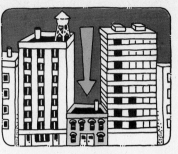

7. promotions/difficult   **8.** training/limited   **9.** company/small

Exercises

Read the sentence and then make a new sentence. Follow the models.

NEW SENTENCE

The work isn't too dangerous for him.

The job is too dangerous for him.

1. The work is dangerous, but he likes it.
2. The job is dangerous. He doesn't like it.
3. There's a health plan, but it doesn't pay for dental work. She doesn't like it.
4. She gets two weeks of vacation, but she wants a month of vacation.
5. He is happy with his vacation. He gets two weeks.
6. She works twelve hours a day, and she doesn't like it.
7. He works fourteen hours a day and he likes it.
8. She isn't happy with her job. She started as a clerk and she is still a clerk.

Write a Story

A. Read the paragraph and then write one word in each blank.

Bill _____(1)_____ happy _____(2)_____ his job. The opportunities _____(3)_____ good.

_____(4)_____ job is _____(5)_____ boring and promotions _____(6)_____ not difficult. _____(7)_____

does not want _____(8)_____ quit.

B. Now write a story about yourself or a friend who has a job. Use the paragraph on page 27 as a model.

_____

_____

_____

_____

Getting Ready

1. Remember that when you give the reason for leaving a job, you should be general, not specific. _Working conditions_ is general. _Dangerous work_ is specific.

2. When you give the reason for leaving a past job, write _found_ . . . . When you give the reason for leaving a present job, write _looking for_ . . . .

3. When you write the reason for leaving on an application form, leave out the little words:

> ~~I am~~ looking for ~~a~~ job with better working conditions.

> ~~I~~ found ~~a~~ job with better working conditions.

Tasks

Read the story and then complete the form.

1.   Penny Harris is working as a welder now, but she is looking for another job. On her job now there is no vacation and there is no health plan.

> REASON FOR LEAVING

2.   Tom Garcia has a new job. He makes good money now. He quit his last job because the pay was low.

> REASON FOR LEAVING

3.   Bob Porter wants to quit his job. He wants a promotion, but his company is small. There is no opportunity for training.

```
REASON FOR LEAVING


```

4.   Jean Wong is a bartender now. The pay is high, but the hours are long and the job is boring. She is looking for another job.

```
REASON FOR LEAVING


```

5.   Anita Prados is a file clerk. She was a laundry worker, but the laundry was small and promotions were difficult. She found another job.

```
REASON FOR LEAVING


```

On Your Own

Complete the form for yourself.

EMPLOYMENT RECORD Begin with present or last job first.		
JOB TITLE	**DATES EMPLOYED**	**REASON FOR LEAVING**
	From To	
JOB TITLE	**DATES EMPLOYED**	**REASON FOR LEAVING**
	From To	
JOB TITLE	**DATES EMPLOYED**	**REASON FOR LEAVING**
	From To	

Lesson Six/6

Getting Ready

1. What are the hours like?
   They are long.

2. My hours are too long.
   You should look for shorter hours (than your hours now).

Conversation

Amy: You look a little down. Is the job getting to you?
Jack: I'm afraid so. The hours are too long.
Amy: Maybe you should look for shorter hours (than your hours now).
Jack: Not a bad idea. Can you give me a few suggestions?
Amy: I'd be glad to, but not now. I'm in a hurry. How about lunch tomorrow?
Jack: Sounds good.

1. HOURS

long   short

2. PLACE

dirty   clean

3. WORK

heavy   light

4. COMPANY

far   close

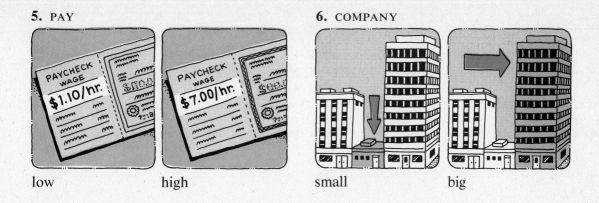

5. PAY

low   high

6. COMPANY

small   big

Exercises

Read about the people. Make questions and then answer the questions. Follow the model. Use these words:

shorter	heavier	farther	lower	smaller
longer	lighter	closer	higher	bigger

QUESTION	ANSWER
Whose hours are shorter?	*Mamie's hours are shorter than Ellen's.*
Whose hours are longer?	*Ellen's hours are longer than Mamie's.*

1. Mamie works seven hours a day. Ellen works eight hours a day.

2. Evo makes $4.50 an hour. Leslie makes $5.00 an hour.

3. David's company is twenty miles from here. Kathy's is thirty miles from here.

4. Wayne's company has one hundred employees. Lisa's company has eighty employees.

5. Martha types from forty to fifty letters at work every day. Alice only types four or five letters every day.

Write a Story

A. Read the paragraph and then write one word in each blank.

Pam _____ unhappy. _____ doesn't like _____ job. _____
      (1)   (2)   (3)   (4)

pay _____ too low and _____ place _____ too dirty. She wants
    (5)   (6)   (7)

_____ pay than her pay now and a _____ place than her
        (8)   (9)

place now.

B. Write a story about yourself or a friend who has a job. Use the paragraph above as a model.

_____

_____

_____

_____

_____

Getting Ready

Sometimes you don't leave a job for personal reasons. You leave because there are things you don't like about the company. When you give the reason for leaving, don't be negative. Don't say things like *My hours are too long.* Be positive. Say things like *I'm looking for shorter hours.*

Tasks

A. Look at the phrases below. In the blanks after each one write *P* for *positive* (good) or *N* for *negative* (bad). Follow the model.

boring work _____*n*_____   light work _____   low pay _____

a clean place _____   heavy work _____   long hours _____ dangerous work _____ high pay _____ short hours _____

a dirty place _____ interesting work _____

B. Look at the reason for leaving the job. Then put an *X* in the correct box. Follow the model.

1. "work was dangerous"
   a. not good; too specific ☒
   b. not good; too negative ☒
   c. good; positive and general ☐

2. "don't like supervisor"
   a. not good; too specific ☐
   b. not good; too negative ☐
   c. good; positive and general ☐

3. "want shorter hours"
   a. not good; too specific ☐
   b. not good; too negative ☐
   c. good; positive and general ☐

4. "place is dirty"
   a. not good; too specific ☐
   b. not good; too negative ☐
   c. good; positive and general ☐

5. "found better working conditions"
   a. not good; too specific ☐
   b. not good; too negative ☐
   c. good; positive and general ☐

6. "pregnant"
   a. not good; too specific ☐
   b. not good; too negative ☐
   c. good; positive and general ☐

7. "want better opportunities"
   a. not good; too specific ☐
   b. not good; too negative ☐
   c. good; positive and general ☐

8. "mother was sick"
   a. not good; too specific ☐
   b. not good; too negative ☐
   c. good; positive and general ☐

On Your Own

Talk to five classmates. You ask questions and complete the form. They answer the questions. Follow the model.

ASK	ANSWER
What's your name?	*My name is Kay Savage.*
What was your last job?	*I was a writer.*
Why did you leave?	*I left because I found a job with shorter hours.*
What did you do before that?	*I was a teacher.*
Why did you leave?	*I left because I found a job with better opportunities.*

NAME	LAST JOB	REASON FOR LEAVING	JOB BEFORE THAT	REASON FOR LEAVING
1. Kay Savage	writer	found shorter hours	teacher	found better opportunities
2.				
3.				
4.				
5.				
6.				

Lesson Seven/7   Review

Check Your Listening

A. Read the questions about the conversation. Listen to the conversation. What did the speakers say? Circle the correct answer.

1. Is Mr. Lee working now?   yes   no

2. Is Mr. Lee an accounting clerk now?   yes   no

3. Was Mr. Lee a mail clerk before he was an accounting clerk? yes   no

4. Was Mr. Lee an accounting clerk for ten years?   yes   no

5. Can Mr. Lee operate any office machines?   yes   no

6. Is Mr. Lee looking for another job?   yes   no

7. Does Mr. Lee want better benefits?   yes   no

8. Does Mr. Lee want to work for a smaller company?   yes   no

B. Read the questions about the conversation. Listen to the conversation again. What did the speakers say? Circle the letter of the correct answer.

1. What are Mr. Lee's duties now?

   a. checks figures and sorts mail
   b. weighs packages and sorts mail
   c. weighs packages and prepares bills

2. What were his duties before?

   a. checked figures and prepared bills
   b. checked figures and sorted mail
   c. sorted mail and prepared bills

3. Which machines can Mr. Lee operate?

   a. duplicator, adding machine, postage meter
   b. photocopier, adding machine, gas meter
   c. photocopier, adding machine, postage meter

4. How long was he an accounting clerk?

    a. fifteen years   **b.** five years   **c.** nine years

5. Why is Mr. Lee looking for a bigger company?

    a. He wants better opportunities.
    b. He wants more benefits.
    c. He wants more pay.

Conversation Review

Find a partner and practice the conversation. When there are blanks, use information about yourselves.

Interviewer: Are you working now?

Applicant: Yes. I'm a _____ .

Interviewer: What are your duties?

Applicant: I _____ .

Interviewer: What did you do before you were a _____ ?

Applicant: Well, in ____*(name of city)*____ I was a ____*(occupation)*____ .

Interviewer: For how long?

Applicant: For _____ years.

Interviewer: What did you do?

Applicant: I _____ and _____ .

Interviewer: Can you operate any machines?

Applicant: _____ .

Interviewer: Why do you want to leave your present job?

Applicant: I'm looking for _____ .

Check Your Vocabulary

Read the sentence, look at the picture, and then fill in the blank.

1. She worked on a farm. She _____ vegetables.

2. Her work isn't interesting. It's _____ .

3. When he was a mail clerk he used a(n) _____

_____ .

4. He was a carpenter. He used a(n) _____ .

5. He _____ lessons.

6. He _____ bar for three years.

Now just read the sentence and fill in the blank.

7. She works from 8:00 a.m. until 10:00 a.m. every day. Her
   hours are _____ .

8. It isn't a big company. There are only six employees. It's a
   _____ company.

9. On her last job she installed and repaired lights. She was a(n)

   _____ .

10. She makes ninety cents an hour. Her pay is _____ .

Check Your Grammar

First read the sentences and then write one word in each blank.

A. 1. I worked for a restaurant _____ 1967 _____ 1971.

2. I was a bartender _____ one year.

3. I was a waiter _____ three years.

4. I have several years experience _____ a mail clerk.

5. I worked _____ a department store _____ a sales clerk.

6. I used equipment _____ tractors and fork lifts.

7. He was a painter _____ December 1972 _____ April 1975.

8. I used to work _____ a school.

B. 1. [sales clerk/1976–1978]   [receptionist/1978–1980]

   _____ she was a receptionist, she was a sales clerk.

2. [counted supplies/1968–1974]   [recorded sales/1974–1979]

   _____ he counted supplies, he recorded sales.

3. [tended bar/1979–present]   [waited on tables/1974–1979]

_____ he waited on tables, he tended bar.

4. He quit the job _____ the pay was low.

5. He is looking for another job _____ he wants a job with better opportunities.

C. 1. He doesn't like his job. He gets three days of vacation a year. The

vacations are _____ short.

2. On her last job she made $3.50 an hour. On her present job she makes $5.00 an

hour. Her pay is _____ now.

3. His company is fifty miles from his house. It is _____far for him. He should

look for a _____ company.

Read and Think

Read the story and then answer the questions.

Employers want information about job duties because they want to know about your skills and experience. On an application form, don't write just one duty. Write all your duties. You should also write the tools and equipment you can use, but don't write all tools or equipment. Only write those that require a special skill.

Read the instructions for the work-experience section of job application forms carefully. Sometimes the form says, *Begin with first job*. But it usually says, *Begin with present or last job*. That's because your present or last job usually requires more skills.

Questions

1. What do employers want information about?
2. Should you write all your duties on an application form? Why?
3. Should you write all tools or equipment?
4. Why is it important to read the instructions on job application forms?
5. Why do forms usually ask for present or last job first?

What Do You Think?

1. Tom is a laundry worker. He sorts clothes. Sometimes he mends clothes too. Should he write *mend clothes* on an application form?
2. Robert is a carpenter. He uses a power saw. He also uses tools like hammers and screwdrivers. Should he write them all on an application form?
3. On Lisa's last job she used a slicer. She didn't like it. Should she write it on her application form?

Put It Together

Fill out the form for yourself.

EMPLOYMENT RECORD	(Begin with your present or last job.)	
NAME OF EMPLOYER	**JOB TITLE AND DUTIES**	
ADDRESS		
NAME AND TITLE OF SUPERVISOR	**TOOLS OR EQUIPMENT USED**	
DATES EMPLOYED From Mon Yr / To Mon Yr /	**REASON FOR LEAVING**	
NAME OF EMPLOYER	**JOB TITLE AND DUTIES**	
ADDRESS		
NAME AND TITLE OF SUPERVISOR	**TOOLS OR EQUIPMENT USED**	
DATES EMPLOYED From Mon Yr / To Mon Yr /	**REASON FOR LEAVING**	
NAME OF EMPLOYER	**JOB TITLE AND DUTIES**	
ADDRESS		
NAME AND TITLE OF SUPERVISOR	**TOOLS OR EQUIPMENT USED**	
DATES EMPLOYED From Mon Yr / To Mon Yr /	**REASON FOR LEAVING**	

Unit 2
Schedules

Lesson Eight/8

Getting Ready

1. How much does it cost?
   It costs $75.00.

2. How are you going to Riverside?
   I am going by train.

3. Are you going by train or by plane?
   I am going by train.   OR   I am going by plane.

Conversation

Anna: How much does it cost to get to Riverside from here?
Jane: That depends. Are you going by train or by plane?
Anna: I don't know. How much does it cost by train?
Jane: (It costs) $75.00.
Anna: And (how much does it cost) by plane?
Jane: (It costs) $100.00. The train is cheaper.
Anna: I want to save money. I'll go by train.

1. train   [$75.00]   plane   [$100.00]   2. streetcar   [50¢]   subway   [75¢]

3. bus   [$5.00]   ferry   [$10.00]

Getting Ready

1. How long does it take by <u>bus</u>?
It takes <u>three hours</u>.

Conversation

Carlos: How long does it take to get to Riverside from here?
Joe: That depends. Are you going by <u>bus</u> or by <u>train</u>?
Carlos: I don't know. How long does it take by <u>bus</u>?
Joe: (It takes) about <u>three hours</u>.
Carlos: And by <u>train</u>?
Joe: (It takes) about <u>two hours</u>. The <u>train</u> is faster.
Carlos: I want to save time. I'll go by <u>train</u>.

 [3 hours]

1. bus

 [2 hours]

train

 [45 minutes]

2. streetcar

 [30 minutes]

subway

Exercises

Read the question, look at the picture, and then answer the question. Follow the model.

[8:00 a.m. – 10:00 a.m.]
[$15.00]

[8:00 a.m. – 11:00 a.m.]
[$10.00]

[9:30 a.m. – 10:00 a.m.]
[75¢]

[9:00 a.m. – 10:00 a.m.]
[$5.00]

1. How are you going to Riverside? *I am going by train.*

   How long does it take and how much does it cost? *It takes two hours and it costs $15.00.*

2. How are you going to Jefferson City? _____

   How long does it take and how much does it cost?

   _____

   _____

3. How are you going downtown? _____

   How long does it take and how much does it cost?

   _____

   _____

4. How are you going to Blue Lake? _____

   _____

   How long does it take and how much does it cost?

   _____

   _____

Write a Story

A. Read the paragraph and then write one word in each blank.

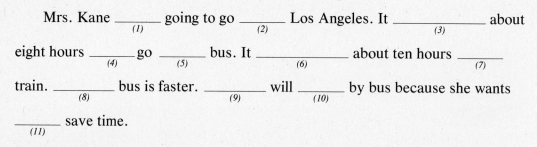

Mrs. Kane _____ going to go _____ Los Angeles. It _____ about

(1)   (2)   (3)

eight hours _____ go _____ bus. It _____ about ten hours _____

(4)   (5)   (6)   (7)

train. _____ bus is faster. _____ will _____ by bus because she wants

(8)   (9)   (10)

_____ save time.

(11)

B. Write a story about yourself or a friend on a separate piece of paper. Use the paragraph above as a model.

Getting Ready

Sometimes the fare on a bus is the same for every stop. But sometimes the fare is different. People who go farther pay more money. When there are different fares for different stops, you need to look at zone charts and fare charts to find the fares.

1.

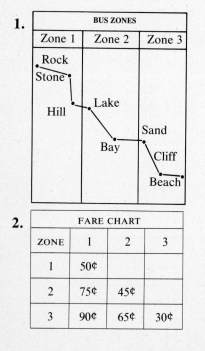

You want to know the fare from the Rock St. stop to the Hill St. stop.

Which zone is the Rock St. stop in? _Zone 1_

Which zone is the Hill St. stop in? _Zone 1_

2.

FARE CHART			
ZONE	1	2	3
1	50¢		
2	75¢	45¢	
3	90¢	65¢	30¢

Find the column with the heading *Zone 1*.

Find the row with the heading *Zone 1*.

Find where the row and column meet.

What is the number in that square? _50¢_

Then the fare is 50¢.

Tasks

Use the zone chart and the fare chart on page 46 to fill in the information below.

1. The Rock St. stop is in Zone _____. The Beach St. stop is in Zone _____. The fare is _____.

2. The Sand St. stop is in Zone _____. The Beach St. stop is in Zone _____. The fare is _____.

3. The Stone St. stop is in Zone _____. The Bay St. stop is in Zone _____. The fare is _____.

4. The Hill St. stop is in Zone _____. The Cliff St. stop is in Zone _____. The fare is _____.

On Your Own

Find out about transportation in your community and complete the chart below.

KIND OF TRANSPORTATION (bus, train, . . .)	NAME OF COMPANY	WHERE DOES IT GO? (inside or outside the city)
1.		
2.		
3.		
4.		

Lesson Nine/9

Getting Ready

1. let's = let us

2. When do you want to *leave from* Elm Street?
I want to *leave from* Elm Street at 3:15.   BUT
When do you want to *leave* New York City?
I want to *leave* New York City at 4:55.

3. When will I arrive *at* Maple Street?
You will arrive *at* Maple Street at 4:30.   BUT
When will I arrive *in* Trenton?
You will arrive *in* Trenton at 5:50.

4. I want to leave at 3:15 this afternoon. When will I arrive?
If you leave at 3:15, you will arrive at 4:30.

Conversation

Carmen: Having trouble?
Alex: I'm afraid so. I can't read this schedule.
Carmen: What are you looking for?
Alex: My arrival time at Maple Street.
Carmen: When do you want to leave from Elm Street?

Alex: (I want to leave) at 3:15 this afternoon.
Carmen: Let's see. If you leave at 3:15, you'll arrive at 4:30.
Alex: Thanks.
Carmen: That's quite all right.

1.

BUS SCHEDULE				
Elm St.	—	—	—	Maple St.
—	—	—	—	—
3:15	—	—	—	4:30

2.

SUBWAY SCHEDULE				
2nd St.	—	—	—	35th St.
10:30	—	—	—	10:40
—	—	—	—	—

3.

TRAIN SCHEDULE				
New York	—	—	Trenton	—
—	—	—	—	—
4:55	—	—	5:50	—
—	—	—	—	—

4.

FERRY SCHEDULE			
Blue Lake	Green Bay	—	—
Lv	Ar	—	—
—	—	—	—
8:25	8:55	—	—

Getting Ready

1. When do you want to arrive <u>at Maple St.</u>?
   I want to arrive <u>at Maple St.</u> by <u>6:30</u> this afternoon.

2. When should I leave <u>from Pine St.</u>?
   You should leave <u>from Pine St.</u> at <u>5:50</u>.

3. I want to arrive by <u>6:30</u> this afternoon. When should I leave?
   If you want to arrive by <u>6:30</u>, you should leave at <u>5:50</u>.

Conversation

Judy: Having trouble?
Paul: I'm afraid so. I can't read this schedule.
Judy: What are you looking for?
Paul: My departure time from <u>Pine St.</u>
Judy: When do you want to arrive at <u>Maple St.</u>?
Paul: (I want to arrive) by <u>6:30</u> this afternoon.
Judy: Let's see. If you want to arrive by <u>6:30</u>, you should leave at <u>5:50</u>.
Paul: Thanks.
Judy: Sure. Any time.

1.

		BUS SCHEDULE			
—	—	Pine St.	—	—	Maple St.
—	—	—	—	—	—
—	—	—	—	—	—
—	—	5:50	—	—	6:30
—	—	—	—	—	—

2.

		SUBWAY SCHEDULE			
35th St.	—	—	—	—	2nd St.
—	—	—	—	—	—
2:50	—	—	—	—	3:00
—	—	—	—	—	—

3.

		TRAIN SCHEDULE			
Trenton	—	—	New York	—	—
—	—	—	—	—	—
12:48	—	—	2:00	—	—
—	—	—	—	—	—

4.

		FERRY SCHEDULE		
—	—	Green Bay	Blue Lake	
—	—	Lv	Ar	
—	—	—	—	
—	—	—	—	
—	—	1:35	2:30	

Exercises

Look at the schedule and then write a sentence about it. Follow the models.

1.

FERRY SCHEDULE			
Blue Lake	Green Bay	—	—
Lv	Ar	—	—
—	—	—	—
8:25	8:55	—	—

2.

TRAIN SCHEDULE				
New York	—	—	Trenton	—
—	—	—	—	—
4:55	—	—	5:50	—
—				

3.

SUBWAY SCHEDULE				
2nd St.	—	—	—	35th St.
10:30	—	—	—	10:40
—	—	—	—	—

1. If you leave at 8:25, you will arrive at 8:55.

2. _____

3. _____

4.

BUS SCHEDULE					
—	—	Pine St.	—	—	Maple St.
—	—	—	—	—	—
—	—	5:50	—	—	6:30
—	—	—	—	—	—

5.

FERRY SCHEDULE			
—	—	Green Bay	Blue Lake
—	—	Lv	Ar
—	—	—	—
—	—	—	—
—	—	—	—
—	—	1:35	2:30

6.

BUS SCHEDULE					
Elm St.	—	—	—	—	Maple St.
—	—	—	—	—	—
3:15	—	—	—	—	4:30

4. If you want to arrive by 6:30, you should leave at 5:50.

5. _____

6. _____

Read a Story

Read the story and then answer the questions.

Mary Katz wants to go on vacation to Pine Lake. There are two ways to get there. If she goes by bus, it will cost ten dollars and it will take two hours. If she goes by train, it will cost twenty dollars and it will take one hour. Mary doesn't know what to do. She wants to save time, and she also wants to save money. So she asks a friend for advice. Her friend tells her, "If you want to save time and money, you should just stay home."

Questions

1. Where does Mary Katz want to go?
2. Is there only one way to get there?
3. How much does it cost by bus?
4. Is it cheaper to go by train or by bus?
5. What is important to Mary?

What Do You Think?

1. If you were Mary, what would you do?
2. What is important to you when you go on vacation?

Getting Ready

1. Here are two ways to read schedules:

   a. These two schedules read from left to right.

FERRY SCHEDULE			
Larkspur	San Francisco		Larkspur
Lv*	Ar*	Lv	Ar
7:05	7:45	7:50	8:30
8:35	9:15	9:20	10:15
9:05	9:50		
10:15	11:00	11:05	11:50
12:05	**12:50**	**12:55**	**1:40**
1:45	**2:30**	**2:45**	**3:30**

BUS SCHEDULE			
8th St.	Main St.	Lake St.	Pine St.
10:27	10:41	10:57	11:12
11:17	11:31	11:47	12:02
12:07	**12:21**	**12:37**	**12:52**
12:57	**1:11**	**1:27**	**1:42**
1:47	**2:01**	**2:17**	**2:32**
2:31	**2:51**	**3:07**	**3:22**
3:27	**3:41**	**3:57**	**4:12**

   b. This schedule reads up and down.

Read Down	TRAIN SCHEDULE	Read Up
4:55 p**	New York	1:55 p
5:10 p	Newark	1:40 p
5:50 p	Trenton	12:48 p
6:20 p	Philadelphia	12:18 p
2:09 a**	Pittsburgh	4:17 a
6:50 a	Columbus	11:25 p
3:50 p	St. Louis	2:25 p
9:20 p	Kansas City	8:55 a

2. On many schedules, 8:50 = 8:50 a.m.   BUT   **8:50** = 8:50 p.m.

---

*Lv = departure time   Ar = arrival time
**a = a.m.   p = p.m.

Tasks

Find a classmate. One asks the question. One looks at the schedules on page 52 and answers the question. Follow the models.

ASK	ANSWER
I want to go from 8th St. to Pine St. by bus. If I want to arrive by 1:30, when should I leave?	*You should leave at 12:07.*
I want to go from Larkspur to San Francisco by ferry. If I leave at 10:15, when will I arrive?	*You will arrive at 11:00.*

1. 8th St./Pine St./bus/arrive 1:30
2. Larkspur/San Francisco/ferry/leave 10:15
3. New York/Columbus/train/arrive 6:50
4. Main St./Lake St./bus/arrive 6:50
5. Larkspur/San Francisco/ferry/arrive 1:00
6. Kansas City/Columbus/train/leave 7:45
7. Pine St./Main St./bus/arrive 3:00

On Your Own

Find out about transportation in your community. Follow these steps.

1. Get two transportation schedules with arrival and departure times.
2. Look at the arrival and departure times. How do you read the schedule? (up and down, or left to right?)
3. On the schedule under *Departures,* find your community or the stop that is closest to your house. When does the first bus (train, . . .) leave from there?
4. On your schedule under *Arrivals,* find your community or the stop that is closest to your house. When does the first bus (train, . . .) arrive there?
5. Give this information to your classmates.

Lesson Ten/10

Getting Ready

1.   fast   faster   fastest

2. Why do you enjoy riding this bus?
It's the _fastest_ bus around.

3. It isn't that _fast_.
It is!

Conversation

Sam: I really enjoy riding this bus.
Lee: Why?
Sam: Because it's the _fastest_ bus around.
Lee: Oh, it isn't that _fast_.
Sam: But it is! Try some other buses and you'll see the difference.

1. fast   **2.** clean   **3.** smooth

Getting Ready

1.   slow   slower   slowest

2. Why do you hate
riding this bus?
It's the <u>slowest</u>
bus around.

Conversation

Lily: I really hate riding this bus.
Pete: Why?
Lily: Because it's the <u>slowest</u> bus around.
Pete: Oh, it isn't that <u>slow</u>.
Lily: But it is! Try some other buses and you'll see the difference.

1. slow   **2.** dirty   **3.** bumpy

Exercises

A. Read the question. Then look at the pictures and the words and use the information to write an answer. Follow the model.

[bus] [subway] [streetcar]

1. Why do you hate riding the streetcar?

It's the dirtiest of all.

[train] [subway] [bus]

2. Why do you hate riding the bus?

_____

[subway] [bus] [streetcar]

3. Why do you enjoy riding the subway?

_____

[streetcar]   [bus]   [train]

4. Why do you enjoy riding the train?

_____

B. Read the question. Then use the information at the left to write an answer. Follow the model.

1. [bus/slow] [subway/fast]   Why do you enjoy riding the subway?

*It's faster than the bus.*_____

2. [bus/slow] [train/slow] [subway/fast]   Why do you enjoy riding the

subway? _____

3. [train/clean] [streetcar/dirty]   Why do you hate riding the streetcar?

_____

4. [bus/bumpy] [subway/smooth]   Why do you hate riding the bus?

_____

5. [train/clean] [bus/dirty] [subway/dirty]   Why do you enjoy riding the

train? _____

6. [streetcar/bumpy] [bus/bumpy] [subway/smooth]   Why do you enjoy

riding the subway? _____

Write a Story

A. Read the paragraph and then write one word in each blank.

Po enjoys _____ the bus. It's the cheapest _____ the
(1)   (2)

fastest of _____. It's a lot cheaper _____ the subway and it's
(3)   (4)

a _____ faster than the streetcar. So Po usually _____ to
(5)   (6)

school by _____.
(7)

B. Read the paragraph and complete the story. Write about what *you* think.

I _____ riding the _____. It's the

_____ of all. It's _____ than the

_____ and it's _____ than the

_____. So I usually go to _____

by _____.

Getting Ready

When you want to know how long it takes to go from one place to another place,
schedules can give you this information.

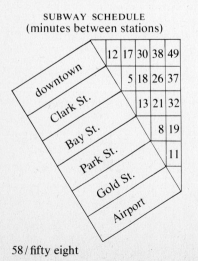

You want to go from downtown to the airport.
Look at the subway schedule. Look across from
downtown and up from the airport. Where do
the row and column meet? What number is in
that square? _____49_____
It takes forty-nine minutes to go by subway.

Look at the bus schedule. When does the bus leave from downtown?

_at 8:05_

BUS SCHEDULE					
downtown	Clark	Bay	Park	Gold	Airport
8:05	8:25	8:36	8:51	8:56	9:01

When does the bus arrive at the airport?

_at 9:01_

How long does it take by bus? (9:01 − 8:05 = 56)   _It takes 56 minutes_

Tasks

A. Read the question. Use the subway schedule and the bus schedule in the *Getting Ready* section to answer the question. Follow the model.

1. How long does it take to go from downtown to Park St.?

   by subway: _30 minutes_ by bus: _46 minutes_

   Which is faster? _The subway is faster_

2. How long does it take to go from Park St. to the airport?

   by subway: _____ by bus: _____

   Which is slower? _____

3. How long does it take to go from downtown to Gold St.?

   by subway: _____ by bus: _____

   Which is faster? _____

4. How long does it take to go from Clark St. to Gold St.?

   by subway: _____ by bus: _____

   Which is faster? _____

B. Find a classmate. One asks the question. One looks at the bus schedule and the subway schedule below to answer the question. Follow the model.

ASK

How long does it take to go from downtown to Front St. by bus?
How long does it take by subway?
Which is faster?

ANSWER

It takes forty-six minutes.

It takes thirty minutes.
The subway is faster.

BUS SCHEDULE					
downtown	Post	Grant	Front	Adams	Beach
8:05	8:25	8:36	8:51	8:56	9:01

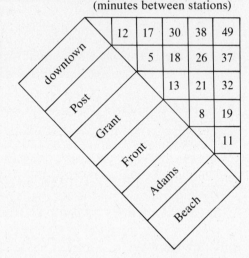

SUBWAY SCHEDULE
(minutes between stations)

1. from downtown to Front St.
2. from Post St. to Front St.
3. from Front St. to Adams St.
4. from Grant St. to Beach St.
5. from downtown to Adams St.

On Your Own

A. Find out about your school or home and tell your classmates about it.

1. Which room is the biggest?
2. Which room is the smallest?
3. Which room is the cleanest?
4. Which room is the dirtiest?

B. Find out about your community and tell your classmates about it.

1. Which building is the biggest?
2. Which school is the biggest?
3. Which building is the newest?
4. Which building is the oldest?
5. Which street is the dirtiest?
6. Which street is the cleanest?

Lesson Eleven/11

Getting Ready

1. scenic   more scenic

2. Shall we go to Lakeside by bus?
Yes, let's go by bus. OR
No, let's not go by bus.

3. Let's not go by bus.
How about going by train?

4. Why don't you want to go by bus?
Going by bus isn't <u>scenic</u>.

5. Why do you want to go by train?
Going by train is more <u>scenic</u>
than going by bus.

Conversation

Tim: Let's go to Lakeside this weekend.
Vic: Good idea. Shall we go by bus?
Tim: No, (let's) not (go) by bus.
Vic: Why not?
Tim: Going by bus isn't very <u>scenic</u>. How about going by train?
Vic: By train? O.K. That's more <u>scenic</u> than (going) by bus.

1. scenic   **2.** convenient   **3.** comfortable

Getting Ready

1. expensive   less expensive

2. Why don't you want to go by bus?
Going by bus is <u>expensive</u>.

3. Why do you want to go by train?
Going by train is less <u>expensive</u>
than going by bus.

Conversation

Lisa: Let's go to Lakeside this weekend.
Jane: Good idea. Shall we go by bus?
Lisa: No, (let's) not (go) by bus.
Jane: Why not?
Lisa: Going by bus is <u>expensive</u>. How about going by train?
Jane: By train? O.K. That's less <u>expensive</u> than (going) by bus.

1. expensive

2. tiring

3. complicated

Exercises

A. Look at the information. Make a question and then answer it. Follow the model.

QUESTION

Shall we go by subway or by ferry?

ANSWER

Let's go by ferry. Going by ferry is more scenic than going by subway.

1. [subway]   [ferry]

2. [train]   [streetcar]

3. [ferry]   [bus]

4. [streetcar]   [bus]

B. Look at the information. Make a question, and then answer it using *expensive, tiring,* or *complicated.* Follow the model.

QUESTION

Shall we go by train or by bus?

ANSWER

Let's go by bus. Going by bus is less expensive than going by train.

1. train/$2.00   **2.** bus/complicated
    bus/$1.00   subway/not complicated

3. ferry/not tiring   **4.** train/$3.00
    bus/very tiring   subway/$1.50

C. Look at the information. Make a question and then answer it.

QUESTION	ANSWER
Why do you want to go by ferry?	*Going by ferry is more scenic and less expensive than going by subway.*
Why don't you want to go by subway?	*Going by subway is less scenic and more expensive than going by ferry.*

1. ferry/scenic/$1.50
   subway/not scenic/$2.50

2. ferry/scenic/not tiring
   bus/not very scenic/tiring

3. streetcar/not comfortable/not convenient
   train/comfortable/convenient

4. subway/comfortable/$2.50
   train/not comfortable/$5.00

Write a Story

A. Read the paragraph and then write one word in each blank.

Ms. Getty wants to _____ to the park this Sunday. _____
            (1)   *(2)*

can go _____ bus _____ by streetcar. _____ by bus is more
         (3)   *(4)*   *(5)*

comfortable _____ going by streetcar. But going by bus is _____
              (6)   *(7)*

convenient than going by streetcar. Ms. Getty does _____ want to
                                                       (8)

walk far. She will go by streetcar.

B. Write a story about where you want to go this weekend. Use the paragraph above as a model.

_____

_____

_____

_____

_____

_____

_____

Tasks

A. Read the question. Then look at the schedules and answer. Follow the model.

BUS FARE CHART						
Between _____ and ____	down-town	Clay	Pine	Smith	Lake	Air-port
downtown	—	.50	.65	.80	.95	1.10
Clay St.	.50	—	.40	.55	.70	.85
Pine St.	.65	.40	—	.40	.55	.70
Smith St.	.80	.55	.10	—	.40	.55
Lake St.	.95	.70	.55	.40	—	.40
Airport	1.10	.85	.70	.55	.40	—

SUBWAY FARE CHART				
ZONE	A	B	C	D
A downtown	.75	.85	1.00	1.25
B Clay/ Pine	.85	.45	.55	.65
C Smith/ Lake	1.00	.55	.35	.45
D Airport	1.25	.65	.45	.35

1. How much does it cost to go from downtown to the airport?

   by bus: _It costs $1.10_   by subway: _It costs $1.25_

   Which is cheaper? _The bus is cheaper._

2. How much does it cost to go from Clay St. to the airport?

   by bus: _____   by subway: _____

   Which is more expensive? _____

3. How much does it cost to go from Smith St. to Lake St.?

   by bus: _____   by subway: _____

   Which is cheaper? _____

4. How much does it cost to go from Lake St. to downtown?

   by bus: _____   by subway: _____

   Which is more expensive? _____

B. Find a classmate. One asks the questions. One looks at the schedules and answers the questions. Follow the model.

ASK	ANSWER
How much does it cost to go from downtown to Beach St. by bus?	*It costs $1.10.*
How much does it cost by subway?	*It costs $1.25.*
Which way is cheaper?	*The bus is cheaper.*

BUS FARE CHART						
Between _____ and _____	downtown	Post	Grant	Front	Adams	Beach
downtown	——	.50	.65	.80	.95	1.10
Post	.50	——	.40	.55	.70	.85
Grant	.65	.40	——	.40	.55	.70
Front	.80	.55	.40	——	.40	.55
Adams	.95	.70	.55	.40	——	.40
Beach	1.10	.85	.70	.55	.40	——

1. from downtown to Beach St.
2. from Post St. to Adams St.
3. from Grant St. to Front St.
4. from downtown to Front St.
5. from Grant St. to Beach St.

SUBWAY FARE CHART				
ZONE	A	B	C	D
A downtown	.75	.85	1.00	1.25
B Post/Grant	.85	.45	.55	.65
C Front/Adams	1.00	.55	.35	.45
D Beach	1.25	.65	.45	.35

On Your Own

A. Get schedules of three kinds of transportation that go to the same place and fill out the chart below.

KIND OF TRANSPORTATION	NAME OF COMPANY	HOW LONG DOES IT TAKE?	COST

B. Now answer these questions.

1. Where are you going? _____

_____

2. Which kind of transportation is fastest? _____

_____

3. Which kind of transportation is cheapest? _____

_____

4. How do you want to get there? _____

_____

Lesson Twelve/12

Getting Ready

1. How often does the <u>subway</u> run?
It runs every <u>fifteen minutes</u>.

2. How often does the <u>subway</u> run during the rush hour?
It runs every <u>fifteen minutes</u> during the rush hour.

3. How often does the <u>subway</u> run after the rush hour?
It runs every <u>thirty minutes</u> after the rush hour.

4. Which runs more frequently, the <u>subway</u> or the train?
The <u>subway</u> runs more frequently than the train.

Conversation

Clerk: Transit Company.
Caller: I'd like some information, please. How often does the <u>subway</u> run?
Clerk: During the rush hour it runs every <u>fifteen minutes</u>.
Caller: And after the rush hour?
Clerk: (It runs) every <u>thirty minutes</u>.
Caller: So it runs more frequently during the rush hour.
Clerk: That's right.
Caller: I see. Thank you.
Clerk: You're welcome.

1.   **2.**   **3.**

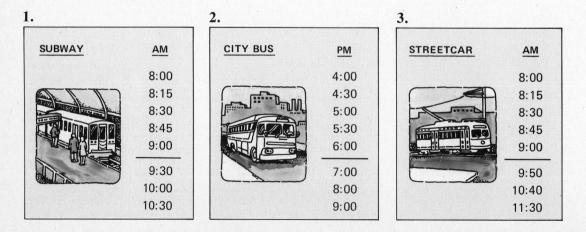

SUBWAY	AM		CITY BUS	PM		STREETCAR	AM
	8:00			4:00			8:00
	8:15			4:30			8:15
	8:30			5:00			8:30
	8:45			5:30			8:45
	9:00			6:00			9:00
	9:30			7:00			9:50
	10:00			8:00			10:40
	10:30			9:00			11:30

Getting Ready

1. How often does the <u>airport bus</u> run on <u>weekdays</u>?
   It runs every <u>twenty minutes</u> on <u>weekdays</u>.

2. Which runs less frequently, the <u>airport bus</u> or the streetcar?
   The <u>airport bus</u> runs less frequently than the streetcar.

Conversation

Clerk: Transit Company.
Caller: I'd like some information, please. How often does the <u>airport bus</u> run?
Clerk: On weekdays it runs every <u>twenty minutes</u>.
Caller: And on weekends?

Clerk: (It runs) every <u>forty-five minutes</u>.
Caller: So it runs less frequently on weekends.
Clerk: That's right.
Caller: I see. Thank you.
Clerk: You're welcome.

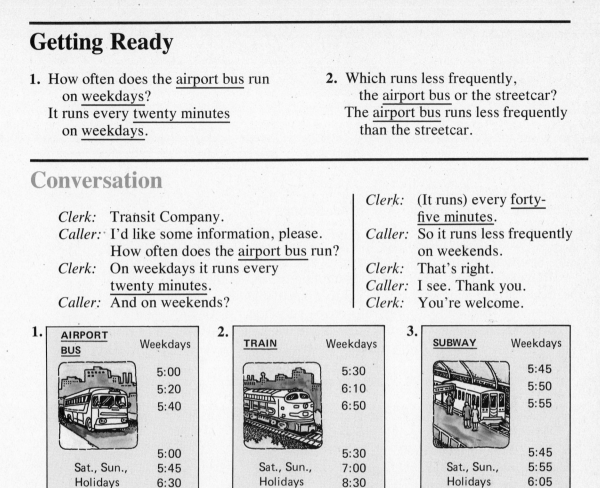

1.
AIRPORT BUS	Weekdays
	5:00
	5:20
	5:40
	5:00
Sat., Sun.,	5:45
Holidays	6:30

2.
TRAIN	Weekdays
	5:30
	6:10
	6:50
	5:30
Sat., Sun.,	7:00
Holidays	8:30

3.
SUBWAY	Weekdays
	5:45
	5:50
	5:55
	5:45
Sat., Sun.,	5:55
Holidays	6:05

Exercises

Look at the schedule. Make a question and then answer it. Follow the model.

QUESTION	ANSWER
How often does the bus run?	*It runs every half hour during the rush hour and every hour after the rush hour.*

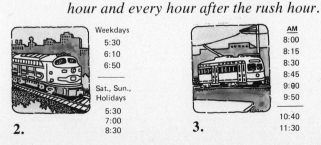

1.
PM
4:00
4:30
5:00
5:30
6:00
7:00
8:00
9:00

2.
Weekdays
5:30
6:10
6:50
Sat., Sun., Holidays
5:30
7:00
8:30

3.
AM
8:00
8:15
8:30
8:45
9:00
9:50
10:40
11:30

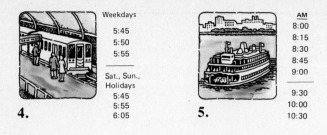

	Weekdays			AM
	5:45			8:00
	5:50			8:15
	5:55			8:30
				8:45
	Sat., Sun.,			9:00
	Holidays			
	5:45			9:30
	5:55			10:00
4.	6:05		**5.**	10:30

Read a Story

Read the story and then answer the questions.

Al Young is looking for transportation to get to work. Time is very important to Al because he doesn't want to be late for work. From transportation schedules Al finds out that the bus is the fastest. It takes fifteen minutes for Al to get to work by bus. But the bus doesn't run very frequently. It only runs once every hour. If Al can't get the 7:00 bus, he has to wait until 8:00 and he will be late. Al will go to work by subway. It takes thirty minutes by subway, but the subway runs every fifteen minutes.

Questions

1. Why does Al Young need transportation?
2. What is important to Al?
3. How long does it take Al to get to work by bus?
4. Does the subway run frequently?
5. How will Al go to work?

What Do You Think?

1. If Al does not take the bus or the subway, is there another way for him to get to work?
2. What is important to you when you go to work?

Tasks

A. Listen to the information about the airport bus schedule. Then write the information in the blanks below.

WEEKDAY SCHEDULE	WEEKEND SCHEDULE
from _____ to _____ every _____	from _____ to _____ every _____
from _____ to _____ every _____	from _____ to _____ every _____
from _____ to _____ every _____	from _____ to _____ every _____
from _____ to _____ every _____	
from _____ to _____ every _____	
from _____ to _____ every _____	

B. Read the question and then use the information above to answer it.

1. How often does the bus run after midnight? _____

2. How often does the bus run in the afternoon on the weekend? _____

   _____

3. How often does the bus run during the rush hour? _____

4. If there is a bus at 3:30 p.m. on a weekday, when does the next bus leave?

   _____

5. If there is a bus at 3:30 p.m. on the weekend, when does the next bus leave?

   _____

6. When does the airport bus run more frequently—from 10:00 a.m. to 3:00 p.m.

   or from 6:00 p.m. to 8:00 p.m.? _____

On Your Own

A. Get a bus schedule, subway schedule, or train schedule. Use the schedule to answer the questions below.

1. How often does it run before the morning rush hour? _____

   _____

2. How often does it run during the morning rush hour? _____

   _____

3. How often does it run after the morning rush hour? _____

   _____

4. How often does it run during the afternoon rush hour? _____

   _____

5. How often does it run after the afternoon rush hour? _____

   _____

6. When is the morning rush hour?   from _____ to _____
7. When is the evening rush hour?   from _____ to _____

B. Now use the answers to write a paragraph about the schedule.

_____

_____

_____

_____

_____

_____

_____

_____

Lesson Thirteen/13

Getting Ready

1.   reliable   more reliable   most reliable

2. How are you going downtown?
   I'm going by bus.   OR   I'm taking the bus.

3. Should I take the bus downtown?
   Yes, you should! It's the most <u>reliable</u> transportation of all.

Conversation

Dick: Say, Jim, I need some information about transportation.
Jim: What do you want to know?
Dick: Should I take the bus downtown?
Jim: Sure, it's great! It's the most <u>reliable</u> transportation of all.

 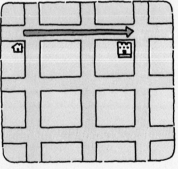

1. reliable   2. direct

Getting Ready

1. reliable less reliable least reliable

2. Should I take the bus?
No, you shouldn't. It's the least <u>reliable</u> transportation of all.

Conversation

Sara: Say, Paul, I need some information about transportation.
Paul: What do you want to know?
Sara: Should I take the bus downtown?
Paul: No, it's terrible! It's the least <u>reliable</u> transportation of all.

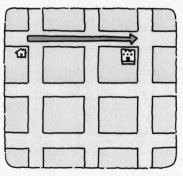

1. reliable

2. direct

Exercises

Look at the pictures and words. Make questions and then answer the questions.
Follow the model.

QUESTION

Which is the fastest of all the kinds of transportation?

ANSWER

The bus is the fastest of all.

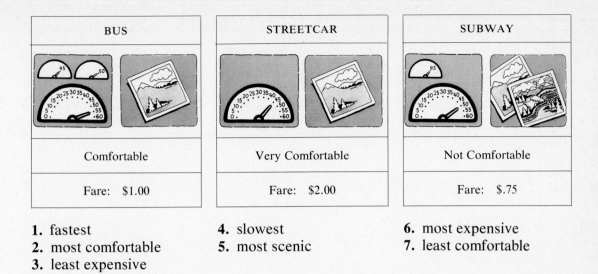

BUS	STREETCAR	SUBWAY
Comfortable	Very Comfortable	Not Comfortable
Fare: $1.00	Fare: $2.00	Fare: $.75

1. fastest
2. most comfortable
3. least expensive

4. slowest
5. most scenic

6. most expensive
7. least comfortable

Read a Story

Read the story and then answer the questions.

Sandy Brown is choosing a way to go to school. She can take the bus, the subway, or the streetcar. Going by bus is the most convenient way because the bus stop is the closest to her house. But the bus is the slowest and the least reliable. Sandy doesn't want to take the bus. The subway is the fastest and most reliable, but the subway station is ten blocks from her house. Going by subway is the least convenient and the most expensive. Sandy doesn't want to take the subway either. Sandy will take the streetcar because it is faster and more reliable than the bus, and it is less expensive and more convenient than the subway.

Questions

1. How many ways can Sandy Brown get to school?
2. What is good about going by bus?
3. What is bad about going by subway?
4. Is going by subway less expensive than by bus?
5. How will Sandy get to school? Why?

What Do You Think?

1. How many ways can you get to school?
2. What do you take to get to school? Why?

Tasks

Listen to the information about the express bus and fill in the chart. Then use this information and the schedules and fare charts below to answer the questions.

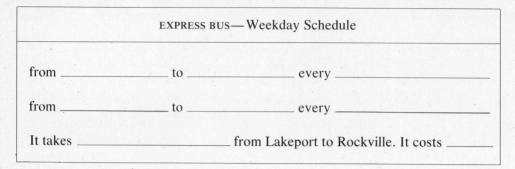

EXPRESS BUS— Weekday Schedule		
from _____ to _____ every _____		
from _____ to _____ every _____		
It takes _____ from Lakeport to Rockville. It costs _____		

FERRY SCHEDULE		
Lakeport	Red River	Rockville
7:00	7:20	7:45
9:00	9:20	9:45
11:00	11:20	11:45

FERRY FARES			
	Lakeport	Red River	Rockville
Lakeport	____	$4.50	$7.00
Red River	$4.50	____	$5.50
Rockville	$7.00	$5.50	____

MINUTES BETWEEN STATIONS

(Trains run every 30 minutes)

	15	30	45	55	75
Lakeport		15	30	40	60
Pineshore			15	25	45
Troutview				10	30
Red River					20
Stone Bridge					
Rockville					

	1	1	2	3
1 Lakeport				
2 Pineshore Troutview		$3.00	$1.50	
3 Red River Stone Bridge		$6.00	$4.50	$1.50
4 Rockville		$10.00	$8.00	$5.00

You want to go from Lakeport to Rockville on a weekday morning.

1. How much does it cost to go by . . . ?

   a. bus _____   **b.** ferry _____   **c.** train _____

2. How long does it take to go by . . . ?

   a. bus _____   **b.** ferry _____   **c.** train _____

3. How often does each run?

   a. bus _____   **b.** ferry _____   **c.** train _____

4. Which one is the fastest? _____

5. Which one is the cheapest? _____

6. Which one runs most often? _____

On Your Own

A. Get transportation information and fill out the chart.

WHERE	KIND OF TRANSPORTATION	COST	HOW LONG IT TAKES	HOW OFTEN IT RUNS
ON VACATION to _____ _____ (place)	a.			
	b.			
	c.			

B. Now tell about three different kinds of transportation for the vacation.

Lesson Fourteen/14   Review

Check Your Listening

A. Read the questions about the conversation. Listen to the conversation. What did the speakers say? Circle the correct answer.

1. Does Mr. Vega go to school by subway?   yes   no

2. Is the streetcar the most reliable?   yes   no

3. Does the bus run the most frequently?   yes   no

4. Is the subway cheaper than the bus?   yes   no

5. Is the subway more comfortable than the bus?   yes   no

6. If Mrs. Kelly wants to save money, should she   yes   no
   take the streetcar?

7. If Mrs. Kelly wants to save time, should she   yes   no
   take the streetcar?

B. Read the questions about the conversation. Listen to the conversation again. What did the speakers say? Circle the letter of the correct answer.

1. How does Mr. Vega go to school?

   a. by streetcar   **b.** by bus   **c.** by subway

2. The bus is:

   a. the most expensive   **b.** the most comfortable   **c.** the most convenient

3. How often does the bus run?

   a. every five minutes   **b.** every fifteen minutes   **c.** every fifty minutes

4. How long does it take Mr. Vega to go to school during the rush hour by bus?

   a. thirty minutes   **b.** forty-five minutes   **c.** an hour and a half

5. If Mr. Vega takes the subway to school, how much will it cost?

   a. 45¢   **b.** 85¢   **c.** 55¢

6. Which is the slowest?

   a. the bus   **b.** the subway   **c.** the streetcar

7. Which is the least expensive?

   a. the subway   **b.** the streetcar   **c.** the bus

Conversation Review

Find a partner and practice the conversation. When there are blanks, use information about yourselves and your community.

You: How do you get to _____? By _____,

            _____, or _____?

Partner: By _____.

You: Why the _____?

Partner: It's the most (or least) _____.

You: How often does it run?

Partner: Every _____.

You: And how long does it take to go to _____

            by _____?

Partner: If I leave my house before the rush hour, it takes about _____.

            If I leave my house during the rush hour, it takes about _____.

You: That's not bad. How much does it cost?

Partner: _____.

You: That's cheaper than the _____. The _____

costs _____.

Partner: The _____ is more (or less) _____ and more

(or less) _____.

You: I want the most (or least) _____ and the most (or least)

_____.

Partner: Then you should _____.

You: O.K. Thanks for your help.

Partner: Sure, any time.

Check Your Vocabulary

Read the sentence and then fill in the blank.

1. It costs 10¢ by bus. The bus is_____ .

2. It costs $20.00 by ferry. The ferry is _____ .

3. The ferry runs every two hours. It doesn't run very _____ .

4. The bus stop is one block from here. Going by bus is very _____ .

5.

TRAIN SCHEDULE				
Trenton	—	—	New	—
—	—	—	York	—
—	—	—	—	—
12:48	—	—	2:00	—
—	—	—	—	—

The _____ time is 12:48.

The _____ time is 2:00.

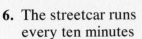

6. The streetcar runs every ten minutes

_____ .

7. The 13 bus is not

_____ .

Check Your Grammar

First read the sentence and then write one word in each blank.

A. 1. How long does it _____ ?

2. How much does it _____ ?

3. It _____ $3.00 by train.

4. It _____ three hours by ferry.

5. How _____ does it run?

6. How _____ does it cost?

7. How _____ does it take?

B. 1. The streetcar is very slow. It's the _____ of all.

2. The subway is very comfortable. It's the _____ of all.

3. Going by bus is not very expensive. It's the _____ of all.

4. Going by train is very tiring. Going by subway is not tiring. Going by subway is _____ than going by train.

5. Going by bus is very convenient. Going by train is not convenient. Going by bus is _____ than going by train.

C. **1.** If you want to arrive by 10:00, you _____ leave at 9:00.

   2. If you leave at 9:00, you _____ arrive at 10:00.

   3. Eight o'clock in the morning on weekdays is _____ the rush hour.

   4. Eleven o'clock in the morning on weekdays is _____ the rush hour.

Read and Think

First read the paragraphs. Then read the questions and find the answers.

There are usually different kinds of transportation that you can use to get around in a large city. You can take the bus or the subway. In some cities you can also take a streetcar. There are also several kinds of transportation for getting around outside of large cities. You can take a bus, a train, or a plane.

How do you decide which kind of transportation to take? First decide what you want. If you want to save money, find the cheapest transportation. If you want to save time, find the fastest transportation or the transportation that runs the most frequently. If you want to enjoy the ride, find the most comfortable transportation or the most scenic transportation.

Look in transportation schedules to find information about travel time and costs. If you can't find the information you need in the schedules, you can also call the transportation companies. If you want to find the most comfortable or the most scenic transportation, you should ask your friends.

Questions

1. What are the different kinds of transportation that you can use to get around a large city?
2. What are the different kinds of transportation that you can use to get around outside of large cities?
3. How can you get information about travel time?
4. If you want to enjoy the ride, should you get information only from schedules?
5. If you want to find out about costs, should you read transportation schedules or should you call the transportation company to get information?

What Do You Think?

1. John needs to find transportation to get to work every day. What kind of transportation (the fastest, the most comfortable, . . .) will he want?
2. Frank wants to find transportation for his vacation. What kind of transportation (the fastest, the most comfortable, . . .) will he want?
3. Norma wants to find the most comfortable transportation. Should she ask her friends for information or should she call the transportation companies? Why?

Put It Together

1. Choose a place to go. Check the appropriate box and complete the sentence.

   ☐ inside your community   ☐ from your community to another community

   I am going from _____ to _____.

2. Next get information about transportation to that place. You can get information from schedules and from friends or people in your school. Use the information to complete the chart below.

KIND OF TRANSPORTATION	NAME OF COMPANY	COST	HOW LONG IT TAKES	HOW OFTEN IT RUNS (WHEN?)

3. Now answer the questions.

   • If you want to be on time every day, which one should you take? Why?

   • If you want to save money, which one should you take? Why?

   • If you want to save time, which one should you take? Why?

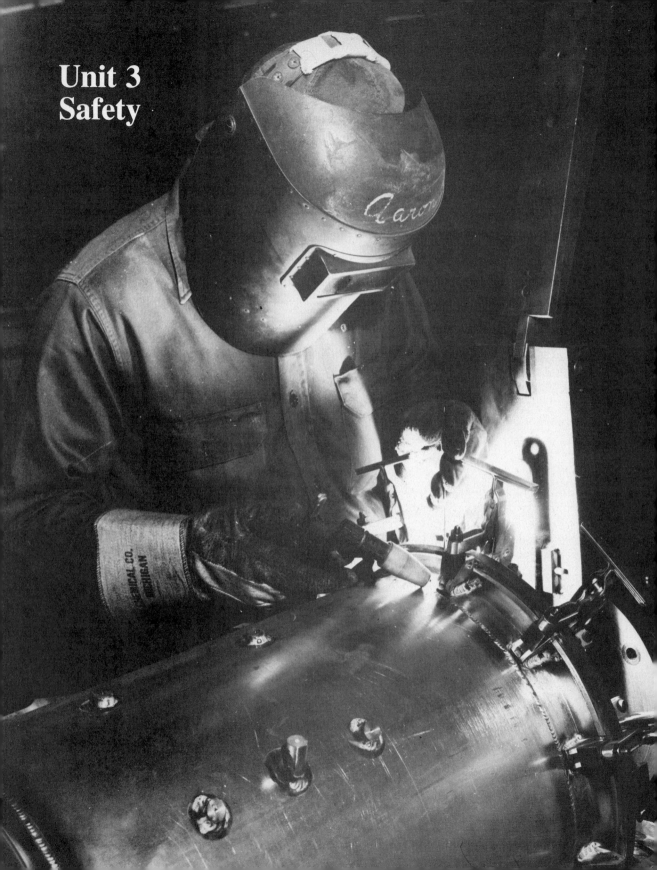

Unit 3
Safety

Lesson Fifteen/15

Getting Ready

1. What kind of safety equipment do you wear?
   I wear a <u>mask</u>.   OR   I wear <u>gloves</u>.

2. Why should you wear a <u>mask</u>?
   It protects your <u>lungs</u> from <u>fumes</u>.

3. Why should you wear <u>gloves</u>?
   They protect your <u>hands</u> from <u>rough objects</u>.

4. *This* <u>mask</u> is important.
   Then I should wear *it*.

5. *These* <u>gloves</u> are important.
   Then I should wear *them*.

Conversation

Old employee: The boss isn't very happy with you.
New employee: Why not?
Old employee: He says you never wear your safety equipment.
New employee: Oh, you mean <u>this</u> <u>mask</u>? <u>It</u> isn't that important.
Old employee: <u>It</u> is. <u>It</u> protects your <u>lungs</u> from <u>fumes</u>.
New employee: You really think I should wear <u>it</u>?
Old employee: I sure do. <u>It's</u> for your own safety.

1. mask

   [lungs]
   [fumes]

2. rubber
   apron

   [body]
   [chemicals]

3. hard
   hat

   [head]
   [falling
   objects]

4. gloves

   [hands]
   [rough
   objects]

5. ear
   protectors

   [ears]
   [loud
   noise]

6. goggles

   [eyes]
   [flying
   objects]

Exercises

Look at the picture. Make a question and then answer it. Follow the model.

QUESTION	ANSWER
Why should you wear gloves?	*They protect your hands from rough objects.*

1.

2.

3.

4.

5.

6.

Write a Story

A. Read the paragraph and then write one word in each blank.

Alicia is ____ (1) cleaning lady. Cleaning ladies ____________ (2) wear gloves to protect ____________ (3) hands from chemicals. Alicia always ____________ (4) her gloves because she thinks they ________ (5) important. The boss is happy __________ (6) her.

B. Write a story about yourself or a friend. Use the paragraph in part *A* as a model.

_____

_____

_____

_____

_____

_____

_____

_____

Tasks

Look at the poster. What safety equipment should the person wear? Why? Write a sentence about each poster. Follow the model.

1.   2.   3.

1. _*She should wear a cap to protect her hair.*_

2. _____

3. _____

4.

5.

6.

4. _____

_____

5. _____

6. _____

_____

_____

On Your Own

Find five classmates. One asks questions and completes the form. The others answer. Follow the model.

ASK	ANSWER
What do you do?	*I'm a welder.*
Do you have to wear safety equipment?	*Yes, I have to wear goggles.*
Why?	*To protect my eyes from heat.*

NAME	OCCUPATION	SAFETY EQUIPMENT	WHY
Amy Adams	welder	goggles	protect eyes from heat

Lesson Sixteen/16

Getting Ready

1. What kind of gloves do you need to wear?
   You need to wear <u>rubber</u> gloves.

2. Why do you need to wear <u>rubber</u> gloves?
   You need to wear them to protect your <u>skin</u> from <u>acid</u>.

Conversation

Supervisor: On this job you need to wear gloves.
New employee: What kind of gloves (do you need to wear)?
Supervisor: (You need to wear) <u>rubber</u> gloves.
New employee: Why <u>rubber</u> gloves?
Supervisor: To protect your <u>skin</u> from <u>acid</u>.

[skin]
[acid]

1. rubber gloves

[hands]
[blisters]

2. leather gloves

[hands]
[heat]

3. asbestos gloves

[hands]
[cuts]

4. cotton gloves

Exercises

Look at the words and the picture. Make a question and then answer it. Follow the model.

QUESTION

Why do truck drivers need to wear leather gloves?

ANSWER

They need to wear them to protect their hands from blisters.

1. [truck drivers]   **2.** [gardeners]   **3.** [hair stylists]   **4.** [welders]

Read a Story

Last weekend Tom wanted to clean his yard. Sometimes when he works in the yard, he cuts himself. So before he worked in the yard, he bought some rubber gloves to protect his hands. After several hours in the yard, Tom's hands really hurt. When he looked at them he saw a lot of cuts. What did he do wrong?

Questions

1. What did Tom want to do last weekend?
2. What does he do sometimes when he works in the yard?
3. What did Tom buy? Why?
4. After several hours in the yard, were Tom's hands O.K.?
5. Why didn't the gloves protect his hands?

What Do You Think?

1. Do all gloves protect your hands from the same thing?
2. What kind of gloves should Tom buy next time he works in the yard?

Getting Ready

Different safety equipment protects you from different things. When you buy equipment, look for special words:

FOR PROTECTION FROM	LOOK FOR
chemicals	acids, alkalis, chemicals
cuts	abrasion, cut
heat	fire, heat

Tasks

Look at the description. Does the equipment protect from heat, from chemicals, or from cuts? Circle the words that tell you. Then check the correct boxes and write the words you circled. Follow the model.

1. | GLOVES Embossed grip. Soft cotton flock lining. "Case hardened" for extra resistance to (abrasion,) (acids,) (alkalis,) salts, ketones.

☐ heat _____
☑ chemicals *acids, alkalis* _____
☑ cuts *abrasion* _____

2. | GLOVES Silvasbestos face, aluminized rayon thumb. The ultimate in glove protection. Designed especially for firefighting, heat hazards, or barbecue.

☐ heat _____
☐ chemicals _____
☐ cuts _____

3. GOGGLES Fogless lens or polycarbonate lens with TLV. For chemical and anti-splash use, plastic hooded vents provide excellent indirect ventilation and protection.

☐ heat _____

☐ chemicals _____

☐ cuts _____

4. GLOVES Gold-colored, heavy-duty. Crinkle-textured coating provides superior grip and cut resistance. Ideal for handling glass, sheet metal, and tin plate.

☐ heat _____

☐ chemicals _____

☐ cuts _____

On Your Own

Look around your classroom, your house, a hardware store, or a department store. Do you see things made of leather, cotton, rubber, or asbestos? List them.

LEATHER	COTTON	RUBBER	ASBESTOS

Lesson Seventeen/17

Getting Ready

1. Should you wear a ring?
No, you shouldn't wear *one* when you use a power saw.   BUT
Should you wear loose bracelets?
No, you shouldn't wear *any* when you use a typewriter.

2. Why shouldn't you wear a ring?
You might catch *it* in the power saw.   BUT
Why shouldn't you wear loose bracelets?
You might catch *them* in the typewriter.

3. What happened?   ⎡ you → yourself   he → himself   she → herself ⎤
I hurt myself.   ⎣ we → ourselves   you → yourselves   they → themselves ⎦

Conversation

Supervisor: Excuse me, _____*(first name of employee)*_____. I'd like to have a few words
with you.
Employee: Is something wrong, Mrs. ____*(last name of supervisor)*____ ?
Supervisor: I'm afraid so. You shouldn't wear a ring when you use a power saw.
Employee: Oh, really? I didn't know that.
Supervisor: That's right. If you catch it in the saw, you might hurt yourself.
Employee: Thank you for telling me. I'll be more careful from now on.

1. a ring/power saw   **2.** a tie/duplicating machine   **3.** a necklace/press

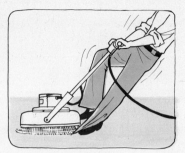

4. loose bracelets/ typewriter

5. loose sleeves/sander

6. loose trousers/ floor waxer

Exercises

Look at the words and pictures. Make a question and then answer the question. Follow the models.

QUESTION	ANSWER
Why shouldn't she wear a ring when she uses a power saw?	*If she catches it in the power saw, she might hurt herself.*
Why shouldn't you wear loose sleeves when you use a sander?	*If you catch them in the sander, you might hurt yourself.*

1. [she]

2. [you]

3. [he]

4. [he]

5. [you]

6. [she]

Read a Story

Read the story and then answer the questions.

      Lynn works in a factory. Everyone there wears ear protectors and aprons. Lynn doesn't like to wear ear protectors because they are uncomfortable. She doesn't like to wear an apron because it is heavy. Yesterday she worked around very loud noise and she didn't wear ear protectors. Today her ears hurt. Last week she worked with chemicals and she didn't wear an apron. The chemicals made a hole in her shirt. That's what happens when people don't wear safety equipment.

Questions

1. Why doesn't Lynn like to wear ear protectors?
2. Why doesn't Lynn like to wear an apron?
3. Why do Lynn's ears hurt today?
4. What happened to Lynn's shirt last week?
5. Why do the workers in Lynn's factory wear ear protectors and aprons?

What Do You Think?

1. If Lynn works around loud noise for a long time and she doesn't wear ear protectors, what might happen?
2. You are Lynn's boss. Are you happy with her?

Tasks

A. First read the question. Then find the answer in the rules and write your answer.

SAFETY DRESS	
RULES AND REGULATIONS	
Things You Should Do	Things You Shouldn't Do
Wear safety glasses when there is danger to your eyes.	Do not wear long, loose hair when you are around moving machinery.
Wear a mask when there is dust or when there are dangerous fumes.	Do not wear loose clothing when you are around machinery.
	Do not wear rings when you use machinery.

1. What shouldn't you wear when you are around machinery? _____

   _____

2. When should you wear a mask? _____

   _____

3. When shouldn't you wear rings? _____

   _____

4. What should you wear when there is danger to your eyes? _____

   _____

B. Find a classmate. One asks and one looks in the safety rules and answers. Follow the model.

ASK	ANSWER
When should you wear gloves?	*You should wear gloves when you handle rough objects.*

1. should/gloves   **4.** should/hard hat
2. shouldn't/gloves   **5.** should/ear protectors
3. shouldn't/tie   **6.** shouldn't/bracelets

SAFETY RULES AND REGULATIONS

<u>Dress</u>

THINGS YOU SHOULD DO

1. Wear gloves when you handle rough objects.

2. Wear a hard hat when there is danger of falling objects.

3. Wear ear protectors when you are in high noise areas.

THINGS YOU SHOULDN'T DO

1. Do not wear gloves when you operate machinery.

2. Do not wear long, loose sleeves or bracelets when you type.

3. Do not wear a tie when you operate machinery.

On Your Own

A. Think about things you do at home and then answer the questions below.

    1. When do you wear gloves?   **3.** When don't you wear loose sleeves?
    2. When do you wear an apron?   **4.** When don't you wear loose trousers?

B. Now find a classmate. One asks and one answers the questions above.

Lesson Eighteen/18

Getting Ready

1. What should you do?
   You should <u>stack boxes straight</u>.

2. What rule is he breaking?
   The rule is "Always <u>stack boxes straight</u>."

3. Why should you <u>stack boxes straight</u>?
   If you don't <u>stack them straight</u>, you might <u>cause an accident</u>.

Conversation

Wayne: Hey, George.
George: What?
Wayne: You know, you're breaking a rule.
George: What rule (am I breaking)?
Wayne: (You should) always <u>stack boxes straight</u>.
George: Why?
Wayne: If you don't, you might <u>cause an accident</u>.
George: O.K. From now on, I'll do that.
Wayne: Good.

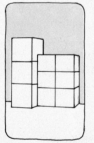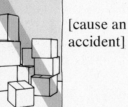 [cause an accident]

1. stack boxes straight

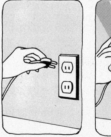 [injure yourself]

2. pull cords by the plug

 [cause an accident]

3. keep drawers closed

 [injure yourself]

4. get help with heavy cartons

 [cause an accident]

5. keep aisles clear

  [cause a fire]

6. keep oily rags in covered cans

Exercises

Look at the picture. Make a question and then answer it. Follow the model.

QUESTION

Why should you always stack boxes straight?

ANSWER

If you don't stack them straight, you might cause an accident.

 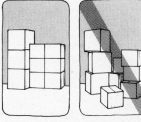

1.

2.

3.

4.

5.

 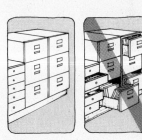

6.

Write a Story

A. Read the paragraph and then write one word in each blank.

Dan works in a repair shop. He _____ to be careful about
(1)

_____ he wears. He shouldn't wear _____ sleeves when
(2)   (3)

he operates machinery. If he catches _____ in the machinery, he might
(4)

hurt _____. He has to be careful _____ things he does.
(5)   (6)

He should get _____ with heavy cartons. If he doesn't, _____
(7)   (8)

might injure himself.

B. Write a story about yourself or a classmate. Use the paragraph above as a model.

_____

_____

_____

_____

_____

_____

_____

_____

_____

_____

_____

Tasks

Find a classmate. Ask and answer questions about the safety posters. Follow the model.

ASK

What rule is the employee breaking?
What should the employee do?
What might happen if employees don't follow this rule?

ANSWER

Always keep . . .

1.   2.   3.

On Your Own

Look around your school, company, or neighborhood. Find two posters. What rules do they show? Tell about the posters.

Lesson Nineteen/19

Getting Ready

1. What's wrong?
   He shouldn't use the outlets.

2. Why shouldn't he use the outlets?
   They're overloaded.
   He might start a fire.

3. When shouldn't you use outlets?
   You shouldn't use outlets when
   they are overloaded.

Conversation

Steve: Look out! You're going to start a fire.
Maria: Oh, come on.
Steve: No, really. Don't use an outlet when it is overloaded.
Maria: Oh, I guess you're right. Thanks for reminding me.
Steve: No problem. Just be glad I'm not the boss.

1. [start a fire]

   use outlets/they
   are overloaded

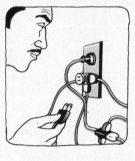

2. [hurt yourself]

   climb on boxes/
   they are unstable

3. [hurt yourself]

   clean machinery/
   it is on

4. [start a fire]

   use cords/
   they are worn

5. [start a fire]

smoke/you are
around flammable
objects

6. [hurt yourself]

use electrical
equipment/you are
standing in water

7. [hurt yourself]

operate equipment/
you aren't
familiar with it

Exercises

Look at the picture. Make a question and then answer it. Follow the model.

QUESTION

*Why shouldn't you smoke
when you are around
flammable objects?*

ANSWER

*If you do you might
start a fire.*

1. 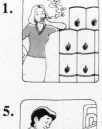 **2.**  **3.**  **4.**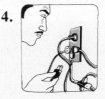

5.  **6.**   **7.**

Read a Story

Read the story and then answer the questions.

Lola works in a plant, but she doesn't like working there. Some of the workers do not follow safety rules about procedures. Last week one worker started a fire because he was smoking near flammable objects. Another worker never closes his drawers. Yesterday the supervisor hurt himself when he walked by the desk. Lola wants to quit because she is afraid she might hurt herself too. She wants to find a new job.

Questions

1. Does Lola work in a safe place?
2. Why was there a fire in Lola's plant last week?
3. Why did the supervisor hurt himself?
4. Why does Lola want to quit?
5. Why is Lola afraid?

What Do You Think?

1. Are safety procedures only for your own safety?
2. What would you do if you worked in Lola's office?

Tasks

A. First read the question. Then find the answer in the rules and write your answer. Follow the model.

SAFETY PROCEDURES	
<u>Do</u>	<u>Don't</u>
Close desk and file drawers when you are not using them.	Do not climb on things like books and chairs.
Pull electric cords by the plug, not by the wire.	Do not stand on wet floors when you use electrical equipment.
Keep aisles clear.	Do not operate equipment when you are not familiar with it.

1. When shouldn't you operate equipment? *You shouldn't operate equipment when you are not familiar with it.*

2. What shouldn't you pull by the wire? _____

_____

3. When should you close desk and file drawers? _____

_____

4. What shouldn't you climb on? _____

_____

5. When shouldn't you stand on wet floors? _____

_____

6. What should you keep clear? _____

_____

B. Find a classmate. One asks and one looks in the safety rules and answers. Follow the model.

ASK	ANSWER
When shouldn't you repair machinery?	*You shouldn't repair machinery when it is running.**

SAFETY PROCEDURES

Keep oily and paint-soaked rags in covered metal waste cans.

Do not smoke when you are around flammable objects.

Get help when you need to carry heavy objects.

Do not clear or repair machinery when it is running.

Stack boxes straight.

Do not overload electrical outlets.

---

1. When shouldn't you repair machinery?
2. What shouldn't you overload?
3. When should you get help?
4. What should you keep in covered metal cans?
5. What should you stack straight?
6. When shouldn't you smoke?

---

*is running = is on

On Your Own

A. Complete the form below.

SAFETY QUESTIONS	YES	NO
1. Do you smoke in bed?		
2. Do you overload your outlets?		
3. Do you store papers near fire?		
4. Do you use electrical equipment when your hands are wet?		
5. Do you use worn electrical cords?		
6. Do you get help with heavy things?		
7. Do you use electrical equipment when you are standing in water?		

B. Now tell your classmates what you do wrong.

Lesson Twenty/20

Getting Ready

1. What kind of supplies do we use?
   We use supplies like <u>rubber cement</u>.

2. Does <u>rubber cement</u> need
   special handling?
   Yes, it does. It's <u>flammable</u>.

3. How should you handle
   <u>rubber cement</u>?
   Don't <u>store</u> it <u>near heat</u>.

4. What might happen if you <u>store</u>
   <u>rubber cement</u> <u>near heat</u>?
   It might <u>catch fire</u>.

Conversation

Old employee:	Some supplies need special handling.
New employee:	What kind of supplies?
Old employee:	<u>Flammable</u> supplies like <u>rubber cement</u>.
New employee:	How should I handle <u>rubber cement</u>?
Old employee:	Don't <u>store</u> it <u>near heat</u>. If you do, it might <u>catch fire</u>.

  [catch fire]     [catch fire]

1. flammable   rubber cement   2. flammable   gasoline

  [burn you]     [burn you]

3. corrosive   bleach   4. corrosive   acid

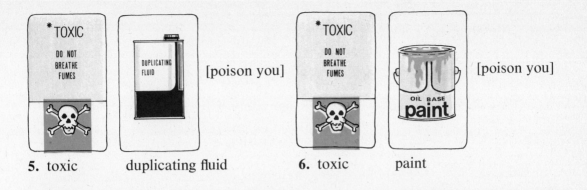

5. toxic   duplicating fluid   [poison you]

6. toxic   paint   [poison you]

Exercises

Look at the picture. Make a question and then answer it. Follow the model.

QUESTION	ANSWER
How should you handle rubber cement?	*You shouldn't store it near heat because it's flammable.*

1.

2.

3.

4.

5.

6.

Write a Story

A. Read the paragraph and then write one word in each blank.

Pam works in a beauty shop. There are safety _____ about things (1)

she uses. _____ like bleach are corrosive. If _____ gets bleach (2)   (3)

on her skin, _____ might burn her. There are _____ rules about (4)   (5)

things she _____. She should wear rubber gloves _____ she (6)   (7)

bleaches hair. They protect _____ hands from chemicals. There _____ (8)   (9)

safety rules about things she _____. She should pull cords by _____ (10)   (11)

plug. If she doesn't, she might hurt _____. (12)

B. Write a story about yourself, a classmate, or a friend. Use the paragraph above as a model.

_____

_____

_____

_____

_____

_____

_____

_____

Getting Ready

Many products are dangerous. If the product is dangerous, the label says, "Do not . . . ."

1. Labels on flammable products have words like *heat, spark,* and *flame.*

2. Labels on toxic products have words like *breathe* and *swallow.*

3. Labels on corrosive products have words like *skin* and *eyes.*

Tasks

Look at the labels. Is the product flammable, toxic, or corrosive? Circle the words that tell you. Then put an *X* in the correct box(es) and write the words you circled. Follow the model.

1. CAUTION. Do not store or use near heat or flame. Use in well-ventilated area. Avoid prolonged breathing of vapor. Avoid contact with eyes or prolonged contact with skin. If swallowed give one or two glasses of water or milk.

   [X] flammable *heat, flame*

   [X] toxic *breathing, swallowed*

   [X] corrosive *eyes, skin*

2. DANGER! Causes severe burns to skin and eyes. Do not get in eyes, on skin, on clothing. When handling, wear goggles or face shield.

   [ ] flammable _____

   [ ] toxic _____

   [ ] corrosive _____

3. CAUTION! COMBUSTIBLE! Contains petroleum distillate. Keep away from heat and open flame. Avoid breathing of vapor or spray mist and prolonged contact with skin. Keep container closed when not in use. Harmful if swallowed.

   [ ] flammable _____

   [ ] toxic _____

   [ ] corrosive _____

4. DANGER! Flammable. Harmful if inhaled. May be fatal or cause blindness if swallowed. Avoid breathing. Use with adequate ventilation. Keep away from heat, sparks, and open flame. Keep container closed.

   [ ] flammable _____

   [ ] toxic _____

   [ ] corrosive _____

5.

> WARNING—Combustible mixture. Do not spray into or near open flame. Harmful if swallowed, inhaled, or absorbed through skin. Avoid breathing spray mist and contact with skin, eyes, clothing. Provide adequate ventilation.

☐ flammable _____

_____

☐ toxic _____

_____

☐ corrosive _____

_____

6.

> CAUTION: Harmful if swallowed. Irritant. Avoid contact with eyes and prolonged contact with skin. Do not swallow.

☐ flammable _____

_____

☐ toxic _____

_____

☐ corrosive _____

_____

On Your Own

Use the information on the labels of products in your home or in stores to complete the chart below.

TYPE OF PRODUCT	BRAND NAME	WORDS ON LABEL	DANGER
hair spray			
oven cleaner			
toilet bowl cleaner			
insect killer			
furniture polish			

Lesson Twenty-One/21 Review

Check Your Listening

A. Read the questions about the conversation. Listen to the conversation. What did the speakers say? Circle the correct answers.

1. Are both employees new?   yes   no

2. Do they have to wear gloves?   yes   no

3. Are there things they shouldn't wear?   yes   no

4. Do they operate equipment?   yes   no

5. Do some supplies need special handling?   yes   no

6. Do they use bleach?   yes   no

B. Read the questions about the conversation. Listen to the conversation again. What did the speakers say? Circle the letter of the correct answer.

1. Why do they have to wear safety equipment?

   a. to protect their eyes from flying objects

   b. to protect their ears from loud noises

   c. to protect their lungs from fumes

2. When they operate a sander, they shouldn't wear:

   a. loose bracelets   b. loose trousers   c. loose sleeves

3. They might cause an accident if they:

   a. don't stack boxes straight

   b. don't keep the aisles clear

   c. don't close drawers

4. They might start a fire if they:

   a. keep oily rags in covered cans

   b. smoke around flammable objects

   c. use an outlet when it is overloaded

5. What needs special handling?   a. drawers   b. acid   c. paint

Conversation Review

Find a partner and practice the conversation. When there are blanks, use information about safety rules in your company.

Old employee: We have safety rules about things you wear, things you use, and things you do.

New employee: What are the rules about things you wear?

Old employee: You should wear safety equipment like _____ .

New employee: Why?

Old employee: To protect your _____ from _____ .

New employee: What else?

Old employee: You shouldn't wear things like _____ when you _____ .

New employee: Why not?

Old employee: If you catch _____ in the _____ , you might hurt yourself.

New employee: What about things you use?

Old employee: Some supplies like _____ need special handling.

New employee: Why does _____ need special handling?

Old employee: It's _____ , so you shouldn't _____ .

New employee: Any other rules?

Old employee: Always _____ . If you don't, you might _____ .

New employee: Anything else?

Old employee: Don't _____ when you _____.

If you do, you might _____.

New employee: Thanks for all the rules. I know they're for my own safety. I'll be careful.

Check Your Vocabulary

Read the sentences and then fill in the blanks.

 **1.** He is wearing a

_____ .

 **2.** She is wearing safety equipment to protect her

_____ .

 **3.** She shouldn't wear

a _____ .

 **4.** You should always

_____

_____ .

 **5.** He is operating a

_____ .

 **6.** The outlet is

_____ .

 7. This needs special handling because it's

_____ .

 **8.** This supply needs special handling because it might

_____ you.

 **9.** You need to

wear _____ gloves.

 10. He didn't wear gloves. He didn't protect his hands from

_____ .

Check Your Grammar

First read the sentence and then write one word in each blank.

A. 1. This hard hat is important. You should wear _____.

   2. These goggles are important. You should wear _____.

   3. If he wears loose sleeves, he might catch _____ in the sander.

   4. If he wears a ring, he might catch _____ in the power saw.

   5. You should wear your gloves because _____ are important.

   6. You should wear your mask because _____ is important.

B. 1. If you work around chemicals, you _____ wear a rubber apron.

   2. If you work around flammable things, you _____ smoke.

   3. If you smoke around flammable objects, you _____ start a fire.

   4. If you don't wear safety equipment, you _____ hurt yourself.

C. 1. I hurt _____.

   2. She hurt _____.

   3. He hurt _____.

   4. They hurt _____.

   5. We hurt _____.

   6. You hurt _____.

   7. Al and you hurt _____.

Read and Think

First read the paragraph. Then read the questions and find the answers.

Safety rules are very important on the job. They are important for both factory workers and office workers. When you begin a job, you should learn the safety rules right away. There are several ways to find out about them. You can read the rules and regulations in the employee handbook. You can read the posters around the company. You can also ask other workers.

There are three kinds of safety rules: rules about clothing, rules about supplies, and rules about procedures. Rules about clothing tell you about things you should and shouldn't wear. Rules about supplies tell you how to handle dangerous products. Rules about procedures tell you about things you should and shouldn't do.

You should follow safety rules. If you break them, your supervisor will think you are careless and will be very unhappy with you.

Questions

1. When you begin a job, what should you do right away?
2. What are several ways to find out about safety rules?
3. What are three kinds of safety rules?
4. Do rules about supplies tell you how to handle all kinds of products?
5. Why should you follow safety rules?

What Do You Think?

1. Is clothing important for safety in a clerical job?
2. You see a worker who is climbing on a stack of boxes. He is breaking a rule. What should you do?
3. Why is safety on the job important to employers?

Put It Together

Look at the picture below. What safety rules are the employees breaking?

Now give the employees some advice.

1. Name things they shouldn't do. Tell why.

_____

_____

_____

2. Name things they should do. Tell why.

_____

_____

_____

Unit 4
Want Ads

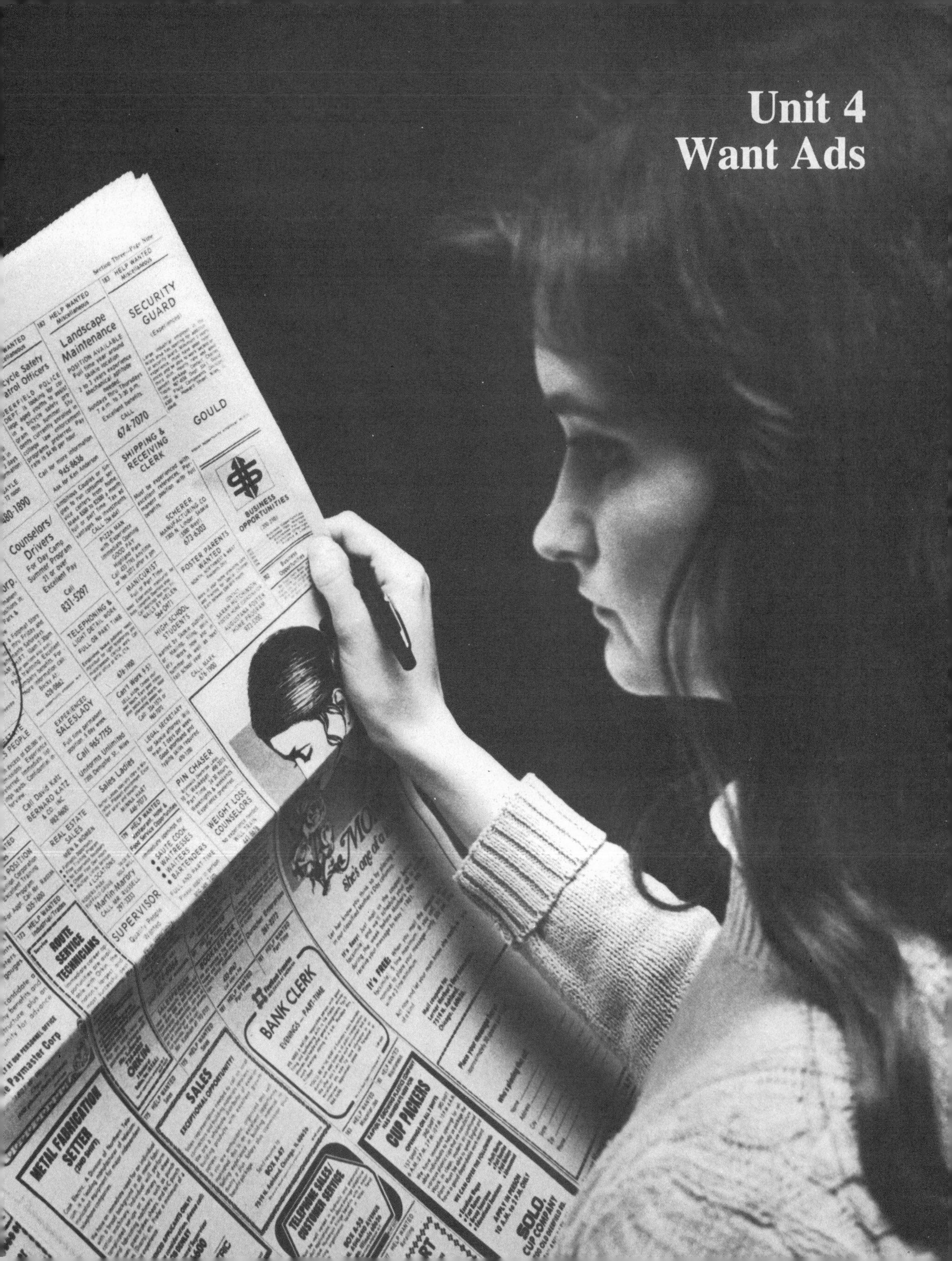

Lesson Twenty-Two/22

Getting Ready

1. What's the job?
   It's a job as <u>an accounting clerk</u>.

2. How do I apply?
   You apply by <u>calling 440-3377</u>.

Conversation

Janice: Hey, here's a job for you.
Henry: Really? What is it?
Janice: It's a job as a(n) _____ (name of occupation) .
Henry: What's the pay?
Janice: (It's) _____ $750 _____ (salary or wage) a _____ month _____ (time period) .
Henry: Sounds good. How do I apply?
Janice: By <u>calling 440-3377</u>.
Henry: Wait a minute. I want to write this down.

1. call 440-3377

2. call the Personnel Department at 864-3579

3. call the manager at 359-9553

4. send a resume to 1330 Broadway Street, Suite 883

5. write to the newspaper, Ad No. 55

6. apply in person at 1550 Adams Street

Exercises

Look at the pictures. Make a question and then answer it. Follow the model.

QUESTION

ANSWER

How do you apply for the job as a welder?

You apply by calling 440-3377.

1.

2.

3.

4.

5.

6.

Read a Story

Read the story and then answer the questions.

Debbie O'Brien is looking in the help wanted ads of the newspaper for a job as an accounting clerk. She found several ads for accounting clerk positions. One ad sounds very good. The duties sound interesting and the pay is good. The ad says that people who would like to apply should send a resume to the company. Debbie is typing her resume now. When she finishes, she will go to the post office and mail it. She hopes the company will get her resume the next day.

Questions

1. Why is Debbie looking in the help wanted ads?
2. What kind of job is she looking for?
3. Are there any openings that she likes?
4. Should Debbie go to the company and apply in person?
5. How should Debbie apply?

What Do You Think?

1. Does Debbie have to type her resume?
2. Why does Debbie want the company to get her resume the next day?

Getting Ready

Look at this help wanted ad and find the job title and the information about how to answer.

Job title

> CLERK Typist—Mailing, filing, and typing exp. req. Knowledge of insurance helpful. Write to this paper, Ad No. 931.

How to answer

Where is the job title? *At the beginning.*

Where does the ad tell you how to answer? *At the end.*

How do you answer the ad? *You answer by writing to the paper, Ad No. 931*

Tasks

A. Read the question and then look for the job in The Help Wanted Ads section of *The Evening Star* (page 164). Follow the model.

1. How do you answer the ad for medical secretary? *You answer by going to Mills Hospital at 100 19th Avenue.*

2. How do you answer the ad for bartender? _____

3. How do you answer the ad for waitress? _____

4. How do you answer the ad for typist? _____

5. How do you answer the ad for medical receptionist? _____

6. How do you answer the ad for X-ray technician? _____

_____

7. How do you answer the ad for upholstery repairer? _____

_____

B. Find a classmate. One asks, one looks in *The Evening Star* (page 164) and answers. Follow the model.

ASK	ANSWER
How do you answer the ad for medical assistant?	*You answer by calling 652-3132.*

1. medical assistant   **2.** receptionist   **3.** secretary

4. gardener   **5.** sales person   **6.** cook

On Your Own

Find three jobs in the help wanted ads section of your newspaper. Put them in the boxes. Then answer these two questions: **(a)** What's the job? **(b)** How do you apply? Follow the model.

1.

> Auto mechanic,
> 1 yr. experience req.
> Gd. pay. Call ~~~~~~~
> ~~~~~~~~~~~~~~~~~~~~
> 943-1043.

It's a job as an auto mechanic
You apply by calling 943-1043.

2.

3.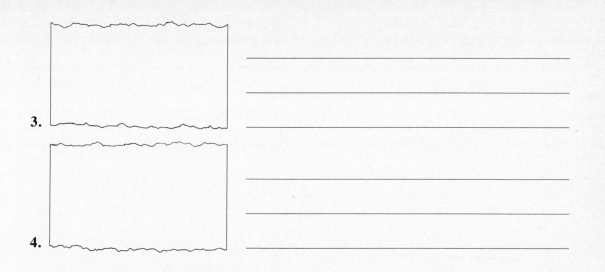

_____

_____

_____

4.

_____

_____

_____

Lesson Twenty-Three/23

Getting Ready

1. What does <u>H.S.</u> mean?
It's short for <u>high school</u>.

2. What does the want ad say?
It says "<u>high-school diploma</u> required."

3. What do you have to have?
You have to have a <u>high-school diploma</u>.

4. What do you have to have before you can apply?
You have to have a <u>high-school diploma</u> before you can apply.

Conversation

Leo: What does <u>H.S.</u> mean?
Carla: I'm not sure. Where do you see it?
Leo: Here in this ad. It says, "<u>H.S. diploma</u> required."
Carla: Oh, <u>H.S.</u> is short for <u>high school</u>.
Leo: Then I have to have a <u>high-school diploma</u>
before I can apply. Right?
Carla: Right.

1. high-school

2. license

3. record

4. references   **5.** experience   **6.** office

Exercises

A. There are many ways to make abbreviations. Read the rule and look at the example. Then write the abbreviation. Follow the models.

1. You can make abbreviations by taking the first letter of each word.

    a. with   *w̶*   **d.** female   _____   **g.** high school _____

    b. full-time _____   **e.** Wednesday _____   **h.** part-time _____

    c. male   _____   **f.** words per minute _____

2. You can make abbreviations by taking the first and last letters of each word.

    a. hour *hr*   **d.** good _____   **g.** week _____

    b. work _____   **e.** room _____

    c. year _____   **f.** light _____

3. You can make abbreviations by taking the first three letters of the word.

    a. reference *ref*   **d.** salary _____   **g.** license _____

    b. office _____   **e.** necessary _____   **h.** answer _____

    c. required _____   **f.** experience _____

4. You can make abbreviations by taking the first three letters and the last letter of the word.

    a. assistant _asst._   **b.** accountant _____   **c.** appointment _____

5. You can make abbreviations by taking out the vowels *(a, e, i, o,* and *u).*

    a. driver _drvr_   **c.** downtown _____

    b. phones _____   **d.** years   _____

6. Sometimes you can make abbreviations by taking out vowels and consonants. Look at the abbreviation. Write the word.

    a. mgr. _manager_   **b.** bkkpg. _____   **c.** ofc.* _____

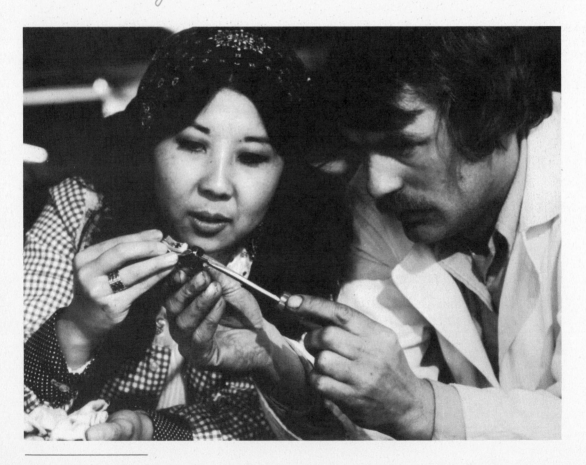

_____

*You can abbreviate some words in more than one way (office = ofc./off.).

B. Look at the abbreviations on the left. Find the full word on the right. Write the full word in the blank. Follow the models.

1. hr.	*hour*	14. m.	_____	**a.**	license
2. yng.	*young*	15. mgr.	_____	**b.**	reference
				c.	assistant
3. acct.	_____	16. nec.	_____	**d.**	office
				e.	appointment
4. ans.	_____	17. ofc.	_____	**f.**	male
				g.	part-time
5. appt.	_____	18. p.t.	_____	**h.**	work
				i.	phones
6. asst.	_____	19. phns.	_____	**j.**	manager
				k.	salary
				l.	equipment
7. bkkpg.	_____	20. ref.	_____	**m.**	accountant
				n.	young
8. drvr.	_____	21. req.	_____	**o.**	full-time
				p.	driver
9. equip.	_____	22. sal.	_____	**q.**	experience
				r.	hour
10. exp.	_____	23. w.	_____	**s.**	necessary
				t.	year
11. f.	_____	24. w.p.m.	_____	**u.**	answer
				v.	bookkeeping
12. f.t.	_____	25. wk.	_____	**w.**	words per minute
13. lic.	_____	26. yr.	_____	**x.**	female
				y.	required
				z.	with

Tasks

Help wanted ads use abbreviations. Look at the ads. Circle the abbreviations. Write the abbreviations and the full forms in the blanks. Follow the model.

TYPIST (p.t.) 55 (wpm,)
$375/month, small
(ofc.) pleasant
working conditions.
398-3444

1. *p.t.*   *part-time*
   wpm   *words per minute*
   ofc.   *office*

TELEPHONE Operator.
At least 2 yrs. exp.
req. Clerical skills
pref. Call 735-0230,
ask for John.

2. _____ _____
_____ _____
_____ _____
_____ _____

SALESPERSON M/F*—
Furniture. Pref. yng.,
aggressive, neat. Sal. plus
commission. 349-2525

3. _____ _____
_____ _____
_____ _____
_____ _____

PLUMBER exp. nec., own
tools and trucks pref.
$10/hr. 661-0871 between
1-5

4. _____ _____
_____ _____
_____ _____
_____ _____

BUILDING Maintenance
Supervisor, must have
gd. driving record w.
valid drvr. lic. Local
refs. req.

5. _____ _____
_____ _____
_____ _____
_____ _____
_____ _____

_____

*M/F = male or female

On Your Own

Find four jobs in the help wanted ads section of your newspaper. Put them in the boxes. Circle the abbreviations. Write the abbreviations and the full forms in the blanks.

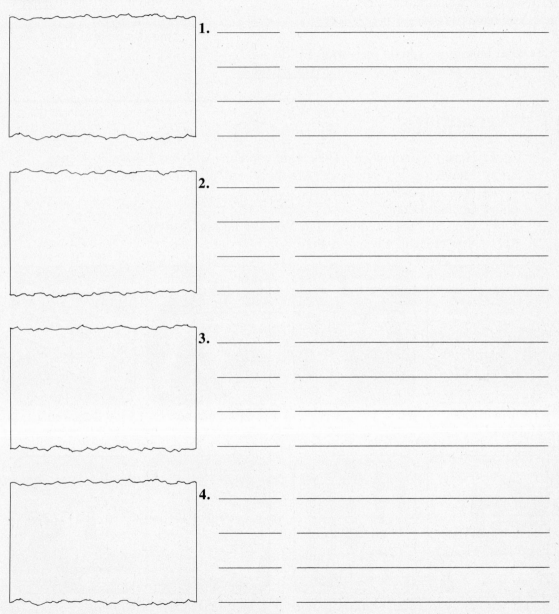

1. _____ _____
   _____ _____
   _____ _____
   _____ _____

2. _____ _____
   _____ _____
   _____ _____
   _____ _____

3. _____ _____
   _____ _____
   _____ _____
   _____ _____

4. _____ _____
   _____ _____
   _____ _____
   _____ _____

Lesson Twenty-Four/24

Getting Ready

1. What are the requirements?
   You have to have <u>a driver's license</u>.

2. Do you have to have <u>a car</u>?
   No, you don't,
     but it's helpful if you do.

3. What kind of person do they want for the job?
   They want someone who has <u>a driver's license</u>.

Conversation

Jack: Here's a job for you. They want someone who has <u>a driver's license</u>.
Lucy: I have <u>a driver's license</u>. (Are there) any other requirements?
Jack: Well, it's helpful if you have <u>a car</u> too.
Lucy: Oh, but I don't.
Jack: Well, it's not a requirement. You should apply anyway.
Lucy: You're right. I'll give it a try.

1. a driver's
   license

a car

2. good phone
   skills

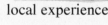

local experience

3. carpentry
   experience

your own tools

4. good clerical
   skills

banking
experience

5. a plumber's   local references
license

6. good accounting   three years
skills   of experience

Exercises

Look at the pictures. Make a question and then answer it. Follow the model.

QUESTION

What kind of person do they want?

ANSWER

They want someone who has a driver's license and a car.

1.

2.

3.

4.

5.

6.

Read a Story

Read the story and then answer the questions.

Tony Vega worked in Mexico as an accountant in a bank. He is now looking for work in the United States. He found an opening for a job as a bank teller in the want ads. The ad says that the teller has to have local experience and local references. It also says that it's helpful if the person has banking experience too. Tony has never worked in the United States, but he wants to apply for the job. Should he?

<u>Questions</u>

1. Does Tony have work experience?
2. Does Tony have work experience in the United States?
3. Which job does Tony want to apply for?
4. What are the requirements for the job?
5. Do you have to have banking experience before you can apply for the job?

<u>What Do You Think?</u>

1. Can Tony get local references?
2. Should Tony apply for the job?

Getting Ready

Help wanted ads give requirements. When you look for requirements, look for the words *must, required* (req.), or *necessary* (nec.).

Ad	Answer
DENTAL ASST., M/F, *must* have X-ray lic. 531-7763	You have to have an X-ray license.
Banking TELLER 1 yr. bank teller exp. *req.* Call Personnel Dept. Toronto Bank. 989-4900	You have to have one year of bank teller experience.
RESTAURANT Help–local exp. *nec.* M/F. Call 845-3009	You have to have local experience

Tasks

A. Find the jobs in the help wanted ads section of *The Evening Star* (page 164).
What are the requirements? Follow the models.

1. gardener _____ *You have to have experience.* _____

2. window cleaner _____ *There are none.* _____

3. PBX operator _____

4. restaurant helper _____

5. key punch operators _____

6. salesperson _____

7. mechanic, elevator _____

B. Find a classmate. One asks about the requirements and one looks in *The Evening Star* (page 164) and answers. Follow the model.

ASK	ANSWER
What are the requirements for kitchen helper?	*You have to have experience.*

1. kitchen helper 2. waiter/waitress 3. janitorial helper
4. bakery counter girl 5. service station attendant 6. auto mechanic

On Your Own

Find three jobs in the help wanted ads section of your newspaper. Put them in the
boxes. Look for requirements. Circle the words *must*, *required*, and *necessary*, and
the abbreviations *req.* and *nec.*

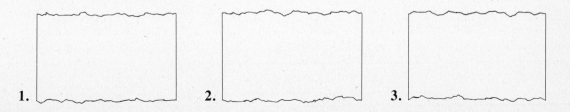

1. ☐ 2. ☐ 3. ☐

Lesson Twenty-Five/25

Getting Ready

1. Are there any openings?
   Yes, there's an opening for a <u>machinist</u>.

2. What are the requirements?
   You have to be able to <u>do repairs</u>.

3. Do you have to be able to <u>read blueprints</u>?
   No, you don't, but they prefer someone who can.

Conversation

Jerry: Here's an opening for a <u>machinist</u>.
Carol: (Is there) any experience required?
Jerry: No, but you have to be able to <u>do repairs</u>.
Carol: Do you have to be able to <u>read blueprints</u> too?
Jerry: No, but they prefer someone who can.
Carol: I can do both. I'm going to apply right away.

do repairs
1. [machinist]

read blueprints

type 65 words
per minute
2. [secretary]

take shorthand

operate a
4-color press
3. [printer]

operate a
cutter

operate a
ten-key
4. [bookkeeper]

handle phones

Exercises

Look at the words and the ads. Make questions and then answer them. Follow the model.

<table>
<tr><td align="center">QUESTION</td><td align="center">ANSWER</td></tr>
<tr><td>Do you have to be able to type?</td><td>Yes, you have to be able to type 65 words per minute.</td></tr>
<tr><td>Do you have to be able to take shorthand?</td><td>No, but they prefer someone who can.</td></tr>
</table>

1. type/take shorthand

~~~~~~~~~~~~~ ~~~~~~~~~~~~ typing 65 wpm required. ~~~~~~~~~~~~~ ~~~~~~~~~~~~ shorthand helpful ~~~~~~~~~~~~~

2. use duplicating machines/ type reports

must be able to type reports ~~~~~~~~~~~~~~~ knowledge of duplicating machines helpful ~~~~~~~~~~~~~~~~~

3. drive/lift 60 pounds

~~~~~~~~~~~~ Must be able to drive ~~~~~~~~~~~~~ ability to lift 60 pounds helpful ~~~~~~~~~~~~~~~~~

4. change oil/do repairs

~~~~~~~~~~~~~~ Must be able to change oil ~~~~~~~~~~~~~ ~~~ ~~~~~~~~~~~ ability to do repairs helpful ~~~~~~~~~~~~

5. operate a cutter/operate a two-color press

knowledge of 2-color press required ~~~~~~~~~~~~~~~ ~~~~~~~~~~~~~~ knowledge of cutter helpful ~~~~~~~~~~~

6. do upholstering/repair furniture

~~~~~~~~~~~ Must be able to do upholstering. ~~~~~~~~~~~~~~ knowledge of furniture repair helpful. ~~~~~~~~~~~~

Read a Story

Read the story and then answer the questions.

Pat Kramer wants to apply for a job as a secretary. She has no experience as a secretary, but she was a receptionist in a doctor's office from 1978 to 1979. She can type fifty-five words per minute and she can handle phones very well. She found two openings in the want ads for a secretary. For one of the jobs you have to be able to type fifty words per minute and you have to have one year of office experience. It's helpful if you can take shorthand too. For the other job, you have to be able to handle phones, and you have to be able to type fifty-five words per minute. It's helpful if you have experience as a secretary and if you have experience working with customers. Which job should Pat apply for?

Questions

1. What are Pat's skills?
2. What kind of work experience does she have?
3. What are the requirements for the first job?
4. What are the requirements for the other job?
5. Does Pat have the requirements for both jobs?
6. What kinds of skills and experience are helpful for the two jobs?

What Do You Think?

1. Which job should Pat apply for? Why?
2. Which job do you think she has a better chance of getting?

Getting Ready

Help wanted ads tell what kinds of skills and experience are helpful. When you look for these skills and experience, look for the words *helpful, preferred,* and *desired,* and for the abbreviation *pref.*

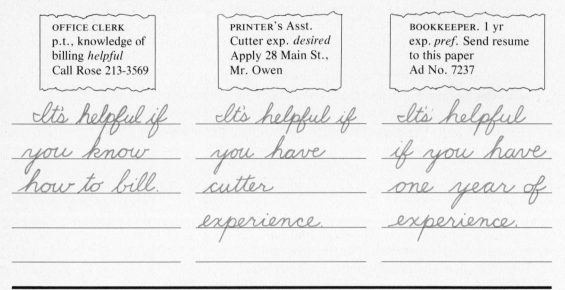

OFFICE CLERK
p.t., knowledge of
billing *helpful*
Call Rose 213-3569

It's helpful if you know how to bill.

PRINTER'S Asst.
Cutter exp. *desired*
Apply 28 Main St.,
Mr. Owen

It's helpful if you have cutter experience.

BOOKKEEPER. 1 yr
exp. *pref.* Send resume
to this paper
Ad No. 7237

It's helpful if you have one year of experience.

Tasks

A. Find the jobs in the help wanted ads section of *The Evening Star* (page 164). What skills and experience are helpful?

1. accounting clerk _____

_____

2. typist _____

3. carpenter _____

4. receptionist _____

_____

5. dental assistant _____

B. Find a classmate. One asks about the helpful skills and experience and one looks in *The Evening Star* (page 164) and answers. Follow the model.

ASK

What's helpful for the job as an electrician?

ANSWER

It's helpful if you have plant experience.

1. electrician
2. bank teller
3. dental receptionist
4. teacher assistant
5. clerk typist
6. plumber

On Your Own

Find three jobs in the help wanted ads section of your newspaper. Put them in the boxes. Look for experience and skills that are helpful. Circle the words *helpful*, *preferred*, and *desired*, and the abbreviation *pref*.

1.   2.   3.

Lesson Twenty-Six/26

Getting Ready

1. What are the requirements?
   You have to be <u>bilingual</u>.

2. You have to be <u>bilingual</u>. Are you?
   Yes, I am.   OR   No, I'm not.

3. Do you have to be <u>bilingual</u>?
   No, you don't, but it's helpful if you
   are.

4. Why aren't you qualified for the job?
   I'm not qualified because I'm not
   <u>bilingual</u>.

Conversation

Jack: (Do you) see anything interesting?
Amy: Yes. Here's something. But I'm afraid I'm not qualified.
Jack: Why not?
Amy: Because you have to be <u>bilingual</u> and I'm not.
Jack: That's too bad. Don't give up. You'll find something else.

1. bilingual

2. accurate

3. over 21

4. good at drawing

5. good at figures

6. good at selling

Exercises

Look at the ad. Make two questions and then answer them. Follow the model.

QUESTION	ANSWER
What are the requirements for the job as medical assistant?	*You have to be bilingual.*
Is Mary qualified for the job?	*Yes, she is bilingual.*

MEDICAL ASSISTANT ∿∿∿ ∿∿∿∿∿∿∿∿ Must be bilingual ∿∿∿∿∿∿ Call Rose 771-3800 ext 29	**RECEPTIONIST** ∿∿∿∿∿∿ Must be good at typing ∿∿∿∿∿∿∿∿∿∿∿ Call 359-9553	**CLERK** ∿∿∿∿∿∿∿∿∿∿∿ ∿∿∿∿ Must be good at figures ∿∿∿∿∿∿∿∿∿∿ ∿∿∿∿ 1860 Grant
1. [Mary/yes]	**2.** [Harry/no]	**3.** [Mr. King/yes]
SECRETARY ∿∿∿∿∿∿∿∿ ∿∿∿∿∿∿ Accurate typing required ∿∿∿∿∿∿∿∿ Call Personnel 398-2000	**TEACHER ASSISTANT**, must be good with machines. Send resume to Horace Mann School, 110 ∿∿∿∿ Franklin St. ∿∿∿∿∿∿∿	**BANK CLERK** ∿∿∿∿∿∿∿∿ Must be accurate ∿∿∿∿ ∿∿∿∿∿∿∿∿∿∿∿∿∿ Call 987-6543
4. [Bill White/yes]	**5.** [Carlos/yes]	**6.** [you/no]

Write a Story

A. Read the paragraph and then write one word in each blank.

XYZ Company has _____(1) opening for a teller. They want someone _____(2) has billing experience and who _____(3) good _____(4) answering phones. It's helpful _____(5) the person _____(6) bilingual too. Jerry Harrington _____(7) qualified. _____(8) should apply right _____(9).

B. Choose a help wanted ad from a local newspaper and then write a story about yourself on a separate piece of paper. Use the paragraph above as a model.

Getting Ready

Help wanted ads give requirements and they tell what kinds of skills and experience are helpful.

    a. For requirements, look for the words *must*, *required*, and *necessary*, and for the abbreviations *req.* and *nec.*

    b. For preferred skills and experience, look for the words *helpful*, *preferred*, and *desired*, and for the abbreviation *pref.*

> ELECTRICIAN f.t., lic. req., plant exp. pref. 380-2700

> CLERK filing nec., typing helpful. Apply in person, 2000 Broadway

1. What are the requirements for the job as an electrician? *You have to have a license.*

2. What kind of person do they prefer for the job as an electrician? *They prefer someone who has plant experience.*

3. What are the requirements for the job as a clerk? *You have to be able to file.*

4. What kind of person do they prefer for the job as a clerk? *They prefer someone who can type.*

Tasks

A. Find the jobs in the help wanted ads section of *The Evening Star* (page 164). Answer these two questions: (a) What are the requirements? (b) What kind of person do they prefer?

    1. dental assistant _____

_____

2. upholstery repairer _____

_____

3. medical assistant _____

_____

4. welder _____

_____

B. Find a classmate. One asks about the requirements and the preferred skills and experience. The other looks in *The Evening Star* (page 164) and answers. Follow the model.

ASK	ANSWER
What are the requirements for the job as a shipping clerk?	*You have to . . .*
What kind of person do they prefer?	*They prefer someone . . .*

1. shipping clerk   **2.** printer   **3.** typist   **4.** travel agent

On Your Own

Find three jobs in the help wanted ads section of your newspaper. Put them in the boxes. Then look for requirements and for preferred skills and experience. Circle the requirements. Underline the preferred skills and experience.

1.   **2.**   **3.**

Lesson Twenty-Seven/27

Getting Ready

1. What kind of person are you looking for?
   We're looking for someone who can <u>translate</u>.

2. We're looking for someone who can <u>translate</u>. Can you?
   Yes, I can. I did a lot of <u>translating</u> when I was at the B.I.G. Corporation.

Conversation

Caller: I'm calling about the ad for a clerk
in last night's *Evening Star*.
Clerk: Yes. We're looking for someone who can <u>translate</u>. Can you?
Caller: Yes, I can. I did a lot of <u>translating</u> when I was at
the B.I.G. Corporation.
Clerk: Good. Can you come in for an interview today at 2:00?
Caller: Certainly. I'll be happy to (come in at 2:00).
What's your address?

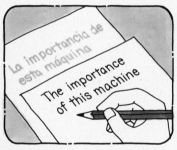

1. translate

2. transcribe

Getting Ready

1. What kind of person are you looking for?
   We're looking for someone who can <u>repair foreign cars</u>.

2. We're looking for someone who can <u>repair foreign cars</u>. Can you?
   Yes, I can. I <u>repaired</u> a lot of <u>foreign cars</u> when I was <u>a mechanic</u>
   at the New Union Factory.

Conversation

Caller: I'm calling about the ad for <u>a mechanic</u> in today's *Evening Star.*

Clerk: We're looking for someone who can <u>repair foreign cars</u>. Can you?

Caller: Yes, I can. I <u>repaired</u> a lot of <u>foreign cars</u> when I was <u>a mechanic</u> at the New Union Factory.

Clerk: Good. Can you come in for an interview today at 2:00?

Caller: Certainly. I'll be happy to (come in at 2:00). What's your address?

1. mechanic/repair foreign cars

2. assembler/assemble motors

Exercises

A. Look at the words and then make a question. Use these words: (a) *can* (b) *is/are* (c) *has/have*. Follow the model.

QUESTION

Is he bilingual?
Can you type?
Does she have local experience?

1. he/bilingual

2. you/type

3. she/local experience

4. you/over twenty-one

5. he/mechanical skills

6. they/repair foreign cars

7. she/good at typing

8. you/handle phones

9. she/license

10. they/good references

B. Look at the word or words. Make a question using "have to." Follow the model.

QUESTION

Do you have to be bilingual?
Do you have to be able to type?
Do you have to have local experience?

1. bilingual
2. type
3. local experience
4. good phone skills

5. lift fifty pounds
6. good at figures
7. do repairs
8. good work record

9. accurate
10. take shorthand

Write a Story

First look at the want ad. Then use the information to write a story. Follow the model.

SECRETARY------
must type 70 wpm,
3 yrs. exp. req.
gd. at figures pref.

1. *Here's an opening for a secretary. They want someone who can type seventy words per minute, who has three years of experience, and who is good at figures. You don't have to be good at figures, but you have a better chance if you are.*

DRIVER-----
loc. exp. nec., must be
over 25, helpful if
can drive truck

2. _____

```
ACCOUNTING CLERK----
must use calculator
insurance exp. nec.,
gd. at typing pref.
```

3. _____

_____

_____

_____

_____

_____

```
MECHANIC------
mech. exp. req.,
must read blueprints,
loc. ref. pref.
```

4. _____

_____

_____

_____

_____

_____

```
CARPENTER-----
must build shelves,
must build cabinets,
car helpful
```

5. _____

_____

_____

_____

_____

_____

Tasks

A. Find the jobs in the help wanted ads section of *The Evening Star* (page 164). List what is required and what is preferred. Then answer these questions about the ads: (a) What kind of person do they want? (b) Are they all requirements? Follow the model.

> CLERK/typist Must be accurate. Bilingual Sp/Eng pref. Apply 2200 W. 19th.

1. clerk/typist

req: _accurate typist_

pref: _bilingual, Spanish/English_

They want someone who is an accurate typist and who is bilingual in Spanish and English. No, you don't have to be bilingual.

2. bartender

req: _____ pref: _____

_____

_____

_____

3. cashier

req: _____ pref: _____

_____

_____

_____

4. secretary

req: _____   pref: _____

_____

_____

_____

_____

5. cab driver

req: _____   pref: _____

_____

_____

_____

_____

6. hotel desk clerk

req: _____   pref: _____

_____

_____

_____

7. travel agent

req: _____   pref: _____

_____

_____

_____

B. Find a classmate. One asks and one looks in *The Evening Star* (page 164) and answers. Follow the model.

<table>
<tr><td align="center">ASK</td><td align="center">ANSWER</td></tr>
<tr><td>What kind of person do they want for the job as an X-ray technician? Are they all requirements?</td><td>They want someone who has a license and who has one year of experience. No, you don't have to have experience.</td></tr>
</table>

1. X-ray technician   **2.** dancers   **3.** bookkeeper   **4.** billing clerk
5. truck driver   **6.** assembler   **7.** painter

On Your Own

Find two jobs in the help wanted ads section of your newspaper. Put them in the boxes. Look for the requirements and for the experience and skills that are helpful.

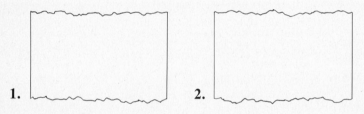

1.   **2.**

Now tell the class about your ads. What kind of person do they want for the job? Are they all requirements?

Lesson Twenty-Eight/28 Review

Check Your Listening

A. Read the questions about the conversation. Listen to the conversation. What did the speakers say? Circle the correct answer.

1. Is Nina looking for a job?   yes   no
2. Does Rick want a full-time job?   yes   no
3. Does Rick want a job as a typist?   yes   no
4. Does Nina know of any openings?   yes   no
5. Is banking experience required?   yes   no
6. Can Rick take shorthand?   yes   no
7. Should Rick apply by calling?   yes   no
8. Is Rick interested in the job?   yes   no

B. Read the questions about the conversation. Listen to the conversation again. What did the speakers say? Circle the letter of the correct answer.

1. What kind of a job is Rick looking for?

   a. permanent   **b.** part-time   **c.** full-time

2. What kind of a job opening does Nina's company have?

   a. receptionist   **b.** secretary   **c.** mail clerk

3. Which one of these things is a requirement for the job?

   a. must be able   **b.** must have   **c.** must be good at
   to type 75 wpm   driver's license   taking shorthand

4. What can Rick do?

   a. type fast   **b.** keep books   **c.** sell insurance

5. What is Rick good at?

   a. figures   **b.** answering phones   **c.** filing

6. How should Rick apply for the job?

   a. by calling   **b.** by going in person   **c.** by sending a resume

Conversation Review

Find a partner and practice the conversation. When there are blanks, answer for yourself.

You: I'm looking for a job as a _____.

Partner: _____ or _____?

You: _____. Do you know of any openings?

Partner: You're in luck. My _____ has an opening for a _____.

You: That's great. What are the job requirements?

Partner: Well, you have to be able to _____.

You: I _____.

Partner: Then you have to have _____.

You: I _____.

Partner: You also have to be _____.

You: I _____. Any other requirements?

Partner: It's helpful if you _____ too.

You: Oh, I _____.

Partner: But it's not a requirement, so you should apply anyway.

You: How do I apply?

Partner: By _____.

You: Thanks. I really appreciate the information.

Partner: Oh, any time. _____ right away and let me know what happens.

You: I will. Thanks.

Check Your Vocabulary

Read the sentence, look at the picture, and then fill in the blanks.

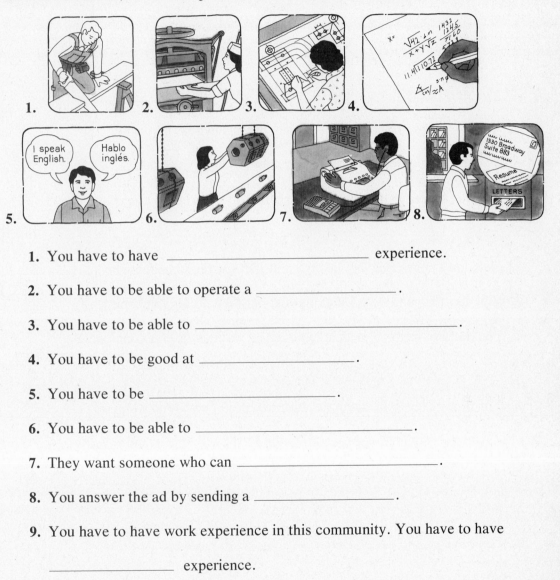

1. You have to have _____ experience.

2. You have to be able to operate a _____ .

3. You have to be able to _____ .

4. You have to be good at _____ .

5. You have to be _____ .

6. You have to be able to _____ .

7. They want someone who can _____ .

8. You answer the ad by sending a _____ .

9. You have to have work experience in this community. You have to have

   _____ experience.

Check Your Grammar

Read the sentence and then write one word in each blank.

A. 1. You don't have to have a car, but it's helpful if you _____.

2. You don't have to be able to type, but it's helpful if you _____.

3. You don't have to be bilingual, but it's helpful if you _____.

4. You don't have to be good at typing, but it's helpful if you _____.

5. You don't have to have experience, but it's helpful if you _____.

B. 1. You don't have to be able to take shorthand, but they prefer someone who

_____.

2. You don't have to have a license, but they prefer someone who _____.

3. You don't have to be good at figures, but they prefer someone who _____.

4. You don't have to have local experience, but they prefer someone who

_____.

5. You don't have to be accurate, but they prefer someone who _____.

C. First read the sentence and then fill in the blank with one or more words.

1. You have to _____ over 21. _____ you?

Yes, I _____.

2. You have to _____ your own tools. _____ you?

No, I _____.

3. You have to _____ handle phones. _____ you?

Yes, I _____.

4. You have to _____ local experience. _____ you?

Yes, I _____.

5. You have to _____ operate a press. _____ you?

No, I _____.

Read and Think

Read the story and then answer the questions.

One way to find job openings is to read the help wanted ads section of the newspaper. They are in the classified ads. If you find an opening, you should scan the ad for the job requirements. You have to have the required skills and experience before you can apply.

Sometimes the ad lists preferred skills and experience. If you have these qualifications too, you have a better chance at the job. If you don't, you should apply anyway because they are not requirements.

After you match your qualifications with the job requirements, you should scan the ad for the way to apply. Some ads want you to go in person to the company. Some ads want you to phone the company. Some ads want you to write to the company or to the newspaper.

Many people in the United States are looking for work. There is a lot of competition for jobs. When you find a job opening, you should apply right away. If you don't, someone else will get the job.

Questions

1. Is reading help wanted ads the only way to find job openings?
2. You have the required skills, but you don't have the preferred skills. Should you apply or not?
3. What are some ways to apply for jobs?
4. Are preferred skills as important as required skills?
5. Today is Friday. Jack finds a job opening in the help wanted ads. Should he apply today or next Monday?
6. What kind of information do you find in help wanted ads?

What Do You Think?

1. Is it important to do what a help wanted ad tells you to do when you apply for a job?
2. You meet the requirements of ten jobs. You have the preferred skills of only three of the jobs. Should you apply for only those three jobs first or should you apply for all ten jobs right away?
3. Why do employers ask about preferred qualifications?

Put It Together

A. Find a job for Mamie by following these steps:

1. Read the story and answer the questions about Mamie's skills and experience.

Mamie was a secretary for three years at a big department store. She can take shorthand at 90 words per minute and type 70 words per minute. She is also good at figures. She is looking for another full-time, permanent job.

What skills does Mamie have? _____

_____

_____

_____

How many years of experience does she

have? _____

2. Look at the help wanted ads for the required and the preferred skills and experience. Answer the questions.

SECRETARY   Typing and shorthand nec. Insurance exp. helpful. Write this paper ad No. 3486

a. What is required? _____

_____

What is preferred? _____

_____

SECRETARY   shorthand 80 wpm, typing 70 wpm nec. 2 yrs. exp. req. Figure aptitude desired. Send resume to 3600 West 3rd St.

b. What is required? _____

_____

_____

What is preferred? _____

_____

SECRETARY/RECEPTIONIST temp. job, no shorthand req. Must type 65 wpm and must have medical ins. exp. Prefer someone gd. w/phns. Call Ms. Rose for appt. 562-3774

c. What is required? _____

_____

What is preferred? _____

_____

3. Now decide which jobs Mamie should apply for.

  a. Which jobs should she apply for?   Job a   Job b   Job c

  b. Which job does she have a better chance of getting? Why?

B. Find a job for yourself by following these steps:

1. List your skills and experience. _____

_____

_____

2. Look in the help wanted ads section of your newspaper and find three jobs
    you would like. Put them in the boxes.

a.

What is required? _____

_____

What is preferred? _____

_____

b.

What is required? _____

_____

What is preferred? _____

_____

c.

What is required? _____

_____

What is preferred? _____

_____

3. Look at the job requirements and at your skills and experience.

    a. Which jobs should you apply for? (Circle the job.)

        Job a   Job b   Job c

    b. Which jobs do you have a better chance of getting? Why?

333
HELP WANTED

ACCT clerk. Knowledge of 10-key and typing nec., 1 yr exp pref. Send resume to this paper ad no 8239.

ASSEMBLER, electronics, must be able to read blueprints. Call (415) 595-1818, ext 69

AUTO BODY repair person, gd mechanical skills req. Own tools nec. 343-9823 after 5

AUTO mechanic, must have foreign car exp and metric tools. Gd pay, benefits, wkg conditions. 782-2721

BAKERY counter girls. Full or part-time. No exp. req. Will train. 751-7931

Banking
TELLER
1 yr bank teller exp pref. Must have good skills. Call Personnel Dept. Toronto Bank 989-4900.

BARTENDER yng. exp.
441-4112

BILLING CLERK, figure aptitude nec., gd. typist pref., local ref. req. 341-1900.

BKKPR. p/t. 5 yrs exp. req. Must be bondable and have gd refs. Call 929-9369 for appt.

CAB
DRIVERS
Must have Calif. drvs. lic., w/gd rec. Must be over 25 yrs old. Apply in person Mon., Tues., & Fri only. 11th and Harrison.

CARPENTER. 6 yr exp req., lic desired. Call 530-7476 evenings only.

CASHIER, must be bondable, local exp. req. 397-1942

CLERK typist. General ofc. exp. req., knowledge of duplicating machines helpful. Call 362-9209.

COOK, p/t evenings. Apply in person, 8001 Sunset Ave.

DANCERS, over 21. Gd. salary and tips. Apply in person after 4 p.m.
PANDORA'S
2018 Bdwy

DENTAL Asst., M/F, exp req., X-ray lic. helpful. 531-7763

DENTAL receptionist, typing nec., accounting skills pref., 829-7000.

ELECTRICIAN, f.t., lic. req., plant exp. pref. Call 380-2700.

GARDENER, exp. nec. Send resume to P. Kennedy, 272 Post St., San Francisco, CA 94109

HOTEL DESK CLERK, 40 hr wk, NCR 4200 exp. nec. For interview Mon-Fri 2-4 p.m. 474-6464

JANITORIAL, $4/hr., day wk. only. Drvrs. lic. and ref. req. 244-2170

KEYPUNCH operators, 2 yrs IBM 3741 exp. req. 838-9600

KITCHEN helper. p.t., exp. req. Apply 5740 Lake St.

MECHANIC, elevator. Must have h.s. diploma, exp. req. 231-4383

MEDICAL Asst., typing pref., must have X-ray lic. 652-3132

MEDICAL Receptionist, exp. req., must be gd. at typing. Write this paper, ad no. 541.

MED SEC'Y, min 2 yrs exp., dictaphone exp nec.
Mills Hospital
100 19th Ave.

PAINTER, 3 yrs local exp pref. Must have H.S. diploma. Own car and equip. req. Call 876-3252 for interview.

PAYROLL clerk, 3-person office. Reply in own handwriting. Box 80005, c/o The Evening Star.

PBX
OPERATORS
f.t., perm. to work swing shift, 1 yr exp req $4.25/hr. 204-0900

PLUMBERS, service and repair exp. req., must have lic., own tools helpful. 328-2277

PRINTER, $10/hr. plus benefits; must be able to operate 4-color press, cutter exp. desired. Call (714) 899-1731 ext. 20, 8 a.m.-4 p.m. wkdys

RECEPTIONIST/Typist, p.t., must be accurate typist, knowledge of filing and billing helpful. Call Rose at 213-3569.

RESTAURANT Help, American food exp. nec., M/F. Call 845-3009

SALESPERSON, f.t., perm., furniture store. No exp. req. Will train. Call Mr. Wells, 477-2515

SECRETARY, shorthand 80 wpm, typing 70 wpm. 2 yr. exp. req. Figure aptitude desired. Send resume to 3600 W. 3rd.

SERVICE STATION Attendant, local refs. req. Apply M-F, 9-3, 1200 9th Ave.

SEWING Machine Operator, 6 mos. exp. nec. Apply 9 a.m.-4 p.m., 1444 Pine St.

SHIPPING Clerk, Drvrs. lic. pref. Must be able to lift 80 pounds. Apply 370 Market, 1:30-3 p.m.

TEACHER ASST, ref req. exp desired. Send resume to 3001 Harrison, San Francisco 94109.

TRAVEL AGENT, 2 yrs. exp. req., bilingual Spanish/English pref. Call 648-5887.

TRUCK
DRIVERS
Min. 5 yrs exp., gd driving rec. pref. Call 746-7891 from 8-5.

TYPIST, must type 70 wpm accurately. Phn. skills pref. Good sal. and benefits. Call Pam for appt., 568-6277, ext. 48, 9 a.m.-5 p.m., Mon.-Fri.

UPHOLSTERY Repairer, Must be able to sew, cut, and upholster. Local exp. pref. $6.50/hr. See Mrs. Ames, 9000 25th Ave.

WAITER/WAITRESS, local exp. req. Apply in person, 5332 East 10th St.

WELDER, must be able to read blueprints, exp. pref. 989-1393.

WIG stylist, Perm., f.t. 421-9824.

WINDOW Cleaner, wk. all shifts. No exp. req. Will train. 262-9013

X-RAY
TECHNICIAN
p.t., in hospital, lic. req., 1 yr exp. pref. Send resume to Mills Hospital, 100 19th Ave.

Unit 5
The Interview:
Answering Questions

Lesson Twenty-Nine/29

Getting Ready

1. What kind of experience have you had?
   I've had experience as an <u>appliance repairman</u>.

2. How long have you been <u>an appliance repairman</u>?
   I've been <u>an appliance repairman</u> since <u>1979</u>.

3. What kind of things have you done?
   I've <u>repaired dishwashers</u>. (I've installed . . . , I've replaced . . . , BUT
   I've <u>driven . . .</u> , I've <u>sewn . . .</u> , I've <u>drawn . . .</u>)

Conversation

Interviewer: Are you currently working?
Applicant: Yes, I am. I've been <u>an appliance repairman</u> since <u>1979</u>.
Interviewer: I see. What kind of things have you done?
Applicant: I've <u>repaired dishwashers</u> and I've <u>repaired washing machines</u>.
Interviewer: Good. We're looking for someone who has had experience <u>repairing dishwashers</u>.
Applicant: Well, I've had <u>three years</u> of experience, and I've really enjoyed it.

repair dishwashers

repair washing machines

1. [appliance repairman/1979]

install thermostats

install intercoms

2. [electrician/1975]

replace springs

replace padding

3. [upholsterer/1965]

drive 12-wheelers

drive 18-wheelers

4. [truck driver/1978]

sew shirts

sew jackets

5. [sewing machine operator/1969]

draw maps

draw plans

6. [assistant drafter/1971]

Exercises

Look at the pictures. Make a question and then answer it. Follow the model.

QUESTION	ANSWER
Have you repaired dishwashers?	*Yes, and I've repaired washing machines too.*

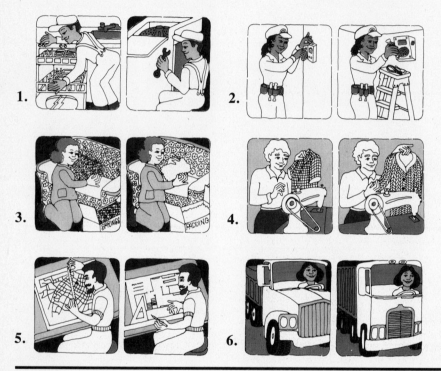

Read a Story

Read the story and then answer the questions.

May-ling Lee has been a clerk in an insurance company since 1977. Now she wants to change jobs. Yesterday she saw an ad for an accounting clerk. They would like someone who has had experience filing, typing invoices, and preparing sales reports. May-ling has some relevant experience* because she has filed and typed letters and invoices. However, she has not prepared sales reports. May-ling would like to apply for the job, but she is not sure of her chances.

---

*If you have done work that uses about the same skills, then you have relevant experience.

Questions

1. How long has May-ling been a clerk?
2. What does she want to do now?
3. What are the requirements for the job as an accounting clerk?
4. Has May-ling ever typed invoices?
5. Has May-ling ever prepared sales reports?

What Do You Think?

1. Should May-ling apply for the job?
2. Are her chances for the job good?

Tasks

First read the questions and the help wanted ad. Then circle any relevant experience on the application and answer the questions. Follow the model.

1.

> SALES CLERK ～～～～～～～～～～～～～
> ～～～～～～～～～～～～～～ Must
> have exp. preparing inventory reports,
> ordering supplies ～～～～～～～～～～
> ～～～～～～～～～～～～～～～～～

What kind of person do they want?

They want someone who has prepared inventory reports and ordered supplies.

COMPANY NAME _____ Co.	DUTIES Stock Shelves Mark Prices (Order Supplies) (Prepare Inventory Reports)
JOB TITLE INVENTORY CLERK	
FROM 7/1/78	TO Present

a. Does this applicant have any relevant experience? *Yes*

Why or why not? *The applicant has prepared inventory reports and has ordered supplies.*

COMPANY NAME	DUTIES
_____ Co.	Clean Floors and Walls
JOB TITLE **JANITOR**	Wax Floors Dispose of Garbage
FROM 1/15/80 **TO** Present	

b. Does this applicant have any relevant

experience? _____ *No* _____

Why or why not? _____ *The*

applicant has not

prepared inventory reports. He has not

ordered supplies.

2.
GENERAL CLERK ~~~~~~~~~~~~~~~~ ~~~~~~~~~~~~~~~~~~~~~~~~~ Must have exp. typing invoices, using duplicating machines, ~~~~~~~~~~~ ~~~~~~~~~~~~~~~~~~~~~~~~~~

What kind of person do they want? _____

_____

_____

COMPANY NAME	DUTIES
_____	Typed Lessons Used Duplicating
JOB TITLE **TEACHER'S AIDE**	Machines Checked Attendance
FROM 8/1/78 **TO** 6/15/79	

a. Does this applicant have any relevant

experience? _____

Why or why not? _____

_____

_____

COMPANY NAME	DUTIES
_____	Received and Recorded
JOB TITLE **SHIPPING CLERK**	Shipments Processed Orders Typed Invoices
FROM 1/15/79 **TO** 4/28/80	

b. Does this applicant have any relevant

experience? _____

Why or why not? _____

_____

_____

COMPANY NAME	DUTIES
_____	Opened and Sorted Mail
JOB TITLE MAIL CLERK	Wrapped and Weighed Packages
FROM 9/21/77 **TO** 1/31/79	Operated Postage Meter

c. Does this applicant have relevant experience? _____

Why or why not? _____

_____

_____

_____

On Your Own

Think of a job that you would like. Find a help wanted ad for that job. Put it in the box. Look for the required experience and then answer the question.

What kind of person do they want?

_____

_____

_____

Now complete this application. Write about your present job or your last job. Then answer the questions.

COMPANY NAME	DUTIES
JOB TITLE	
FROM **TO**	

Do you have any relevant experience?

_____

Why? _____

_____

Lesson Thirty/30

Getting Ready

1. What position are you interested in?
   I'm interested in the position
      as a <u>carpenter's apprentice</u>.

2. How long were you a <u>carpenter's apprentice</u>?
   I was a <u>carpenter's apprentice</u> for two years.

3. Did you <u>build cabinets</u>
      on your last job?
   Yes, I did. OR
   Yes, I <u>built cabinets</u>.

4. Did you do <u>refinishing</u>
      on your last job?
   Yes, I did. OR
   Yes, I <u>did refinishing</u>.

Conversation

Interviewer: What can we do for you today?
Applicant: I'm interested in the position as a <u>carpenter's apprentice</u>.
Interviewer: Have you had any experience?
Applicant: I was a <u>carpenter's apprentice</u> for two years.
Interviewer: Did you <u>build cabinets</u>?
Applicant: Yes, I did, and I did some <u>refinishing</u> too.

build cabinets

do refinishing

1. [carpenter's apprentice]

make suits

do alterations

2. [dressmaker]

Getting Ready

1. Have you had any experience?
   Yes, I've been <u>an</u> <u>editorial assistant</u> for the past two years.

2. Have you ever <u>written copy</u>?
   Yes, I have. OR
   Yes, I've <u>written copy</u>.

3. Have you ever <u>done proofreading</u>?
   Yes, I have. OR
   Yes, I've <u>done proofreading</u>.

Conversation

Interviewer: What can we do for you today?
Applicant: I'm interested in the position as <u>an editorial assistant</u>.
Interviewer: Have you had any experience?
Applicant: I've been <u>an editorial assistant</u> for the past two years.
Interviewer: Have you ever <u>written copy</u>?
Applicant: Yes, I have, and I've <u>done</u> some <u>proofreading</u> too.

write
copy

do
proofreading

1. [editorial assistant]

give
injections

do
scheduling

2. [medical assistant]

Exercises

Look at the pictures. Make a question and then answer it. Follow the models.

QUESTION	ANSWER
How long were you a carpenter's apprentice?	*I was a carpenter's apprentice for two years.*
What kind of things did you do?	*I built cabinets and did refinishing.*
How long have you been an editorial assistant?	*I've been an editorial assistant since 1978.*
What kind of things have you done?	*I've written copy and done proofreading.*

[carpenter's apprentice]
1. [1977–'79]

[editorial assistant]
2. [1978–present]

[medical assistant]
3. [1979–present]

[dressmaker]
4. [1973–'76]

[upholsterer]
5. [1969–'72]

[assistant drafter]
6. [1975–present]

[plumber's apprentice]
7. [1979–present]

[truck driver]
8. [1968–'70]

Write a Story

A. Read the paragraph and then write one word in each blank.

Georgia _____ *(1)* _____ *(2)* a dressmaker _____ *(3)* the _____ *(4)*

four years. She _____ *(5)* made dresses and suits. Before that she

_____ *(6)* a sewing machine operator _____ *(7)* two years. _____ *(8)*

sewed shirts _____ *(9)* jackets.

B. Write a story about yourself, using the paragraph above as a model.

_____

_____

_____

_____

_____

_____

_____

_____

Tasks

Look at the help wanted ad for required experience. Then look at the application forms for relevant experience. Circle the relevant experience and write what to say in an interview. Follow the model.

SALESPERSON Auto parts store. Knowledge of auto parts req., sales and inventory exp. a must

1.

COMPANY NAME	DUTIES
_____	Stock Shelves
JOB TITLE Stock Clerk	(Record Inventory)
FROM 2/1/80 **TO** present	

COMPANY NAME	DUTIES
_____	(Sell and Order Auto Parts)
JOB TITLE Sales Clerk	Stock Shelves
FROM 8/1/79 **TO** present	

COMPANY NAME	DUTIES
_____	Pumped Gas
JOB TITLE Service Station Attendant	Changed Tires and Oil
FROM 8/10/79 **TO** 1/25/80	(Sold and Ordered Auto Parts)

COMPANY NAME	DUTIES
_____	(Sold and Ordered Books)
JOB TITLE Sales Clerk	Arranged Displays
FROM 1/5/79 **TO** 7/31/79	

I have been a service station attendant and a stock clerk. I have sold and ordered auto parts. I have also recorded inventory.

I have been a sales clerk. I have sold and ordered auto parts.

BANK TELLER 〰〰〰〰〰〰〰〰
Must have cash handling exp.
and be able to type 〰〰〰〰〰
〰〰〰〰〰〰〰〰〰〰〰〰〰〰〰

2.

COMPANY NAME	DUTIES
_____	calculate bills
JOB TITLE **CASHIER**	collect cash and make change
FROM **TO** 2/10/79 Present	record and check amounts

COMPANY NAME	DUTIES
_____	sell tickets
JOB TITLE **TICKET SELLER**	collect cash and make change
FROM **TO** 8/15/79 Present	

COMPANY NAME	DUTIES
_____	opened and sorted mail
JOB TITLE **MAIL CLERK**	typed mailing labels and envelopes
FROM **TO** 6/1/78 12/15/78	

COMPANY NAME	DUTIES
_____	stocked shelves marked prices wrapped packages
JOB TITLE **STOCK CLERK**	
FROM **TO** 7/16/78 8/10/79	

_____   _____

_____   _____

_____   _____

_____   _____

_____   _____

_____   _____

On Your Own

Fill out the application for yourself. Now think of a job that you would like. Find a help wanted ad for that job. Put the ad in the box. Then look for the required experience and write what to say in the interview.

COMPANY NAME	DUTIES
JOB TITLE	
FROM **TO**	

COMPANY NAME	DUTIES
JOB TITLE	
FROM **TO**	

COMPANY NAME	DUTIES
JOB TITLE	
FROM **TO**	

Now think of a job that you would like. Find a help wanted ad for that job. Put the ad in the box. Circle the required experience.

Now write what you would say in an interview.

_____

_____

_____

_____

Lesson Thirty-One/31

Getting Ready

1. Have you ever <u>taken inventory</u>?
   Yes, I used to <u>take inventory</u> in a <u>grocery store</u>.

2. When did you work in a <u>grocery store</u>?
   I worked in one five years ago.

3. How often did you work in the <u>grocery store</u>?
   I worked there every other weekend.

Conversation

Interviewer: Have you ever <u>taken inventory</u>?
Applicant: Yes, I used to <u>take inventory</u> when I helped out in my uncle's <u>grocery store</u>.
Interviewer: When was that?
Applicant: (That was) five years ago.
Interviewer: How often did you work there?
Applicant: (I worked there) every other weekend.

   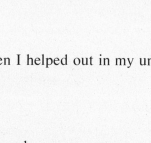

1. take inventory   grocery store   2. sell souvenirs   souvenir shop

3. process bills   flower shop   4. handle money   motel

5. keep records real estate office

Exercises

Look at the picture. Make a question and then answer it. Follow the model.

QUESTION

Have you ever handled money?

ANSWER

Yes, I used to handle money when I helped out in my uncle's motel.

1.

2.

3.

4.

5.

Read a Story

Read the story and then answer the questions.

Mimi Ho is going to an interview tomorrow. This is her first interview and she is worried. She is a good typist, but she doesn't have any paid work experience. When she was in high school she used to help out in her father's real estate office. She worked there every other afternoon for two years. She typed bills and letters and answered the telephone, but her father never paid her for the work. Should Mimi tell the interviewer about her work experience in her father's office?

Questions

1. Why is Mimi Ho worried about the interview?
2. Does Mimi have any skills?
3. Does Mimi have any paid experience?
4. Does Mimi have any work experience at all?
5. What kind of experience has she had?

What Do You Think?

1. Would you hire Mimi as a typist? Why or why not?
2. Does work experience have to be paid experience?

Tasks

A. Read about the applicant. Check relevant duties. Then write what to say in an interview. Follow the model.

1. Pedro Gomez is applying for a job as a sales clerk. He used to help out in his uncle's souvenir shop.

☐ **a.** cleaned the floor

☑ **b.** sold souvenirs

☐ **c.** took inventory

I used to sell souvenirs when I helped out in my uncle's souvenir shop.

2. Erica Petersen is applying for a job as a cashier. She used to help out in her family's restaurant.

☐ **a.** waited on tables

☐ **b.** mixed drinks

☐ **c.** collected money from customers

_____

_____

_____

_____

3. Peter Cook is applying for a job as an accounting clerk. He used to help out in his father's real estate office.

☐ **a.** kept books

☐ **b.** filed reports

☐ **c.** answered telephones

_____

_____

_____

_____

4. John Ma is applying for a job as a carpenter's apprentice. He used to help out in his uncle's furniture store.

☐ **a.** sanded and painted chairs

☐ **b.** cleaned the floor

☐ **c.** drove a truck

_____

_____

_____

_____

B. Listen to the tape. Listen for information about the length of the job and the duties. Then check the items the applicant described and tell which applicant gave a more complete answer.

1.

Applicant A
- ☐ length of job
- ☐ duties

Applicant B
- ☐ length of job
- ☐ duties

2.

Applicant A
- ☐ length of job
- ☐ duties

Applicant B
- ☐ length of job
- ☐ duties

3.

Applicant A
- ☐ length of job
- ☐ duties

Applicant B
- ☐ length of job
- ☐ duties

4.

Applicant A
- ☐ length of jobs
- ☐ duties

Applicant B
- ☐ length of job
- ☐ duties

On Your Own

Have you ever worked without pay? What did you do? For how long? How often?

_____

_____

_____

_____

_____

Lesson Thirty-Two/32

Getting Ready

1. Have you had any experience in
   <u>health services</u>?
   Yes, I've had some.   OR
   No, I haven't had any.

2. Did you take any classes last
   semester?
   Yes, I took a <u>first-aid</u> class.   OR
   No, I didn't take any.

Conversation

Interviewer: I see you don't have any experience in <u>health services</u>.
Applicant: That's true, but I took a <u>first-aid</u> class for two semesters in adult
school.
Interviewer: Why do you want to leave your present job?
Applicant: I've always wanted to get into <u>health services</u>, and this job looks
like a good place to start.
Interviewer: I see. I'd like to check your references. Do you mind if I call your
supervisor?
Applicant: I'd rather you didn't. I haven't given notice yet.

1. health services   first-aid   **2.** construction   mechanical-
                                                                       drawing

3. sales   retailing

Getting Ready

1. Have you had any experience in
 <u>computer operations</u>?
 Yes, I've had some experience in
 <u>computer operations</u>. OR
 No, I haven't had any experience in
 <u>computer operations</u>.

2. Are you taking any classes?
 Yes, I've been taking <u>computer
 classes</u> for the past year.

Conversation

Interviewer: I see you don't have any experience in <u>computer operations</u>.
Applicant: That's true, but I've been taking <u>computer</u> classes for the past year.
Interviewer: Why do you want to leave your present job?
Applicant: I've always wanted to get into <u>computer operations</u>, and this job
 looks like a good place to start.
Interviewer: I see. I'd like to check your references. Do you mind if I call your
 supervisor?
Applicant: Not at all. My supervisor is Mr. Simmons. His phone number is on
 my application.

1. computer
 operations
 computer
2. electronics
 TV repair

3. banking
 bank-teller

Exercises

A. Look at the pictures and the words. Make a question and then answer it. Follow the model.

QUESTION	ANSWER
Did John take any first-aid classes?	*Yes, he took first aid for two semesters.*

1. [John/2 semesters]

2. [Ed/one semester]

3. [Mary/6 months]

4. [Ines/4 months]

B. Look at the picture and the words. Make a question and then answer it. Follow the model.

QUESTION	ANSWER
Has Rita taken any computer classes?	*Yes, she's been taking computer classes for the past year.*

1. [Rita/one year]

2. [John/10 weeks]

3. [Alice/3 months]

4. [Ed/6 months]

Read a Story

Read the story and then answer the questions.

Ellen Kim is from Korea and she is looking for a job as a typist. She has a job interview tomorrow, but she hasn't had any experience as a typist. She is thinking about how to answer questions about her work experience.

After Ellen finished high school in Korea, she didn't go to college. She took some clerical classes in a special business school for one year. Then she came to the United States and has been taking a typing class in an adult school for two semesters. Ellen should tell the interviewer about these classes. They are relevant training for the job as a typist.

<u>Questions</u>

1. What kind of job is Ellen applying for?
2. Why is she thinking about how to answer questions about her work experience?
3. Did she have any relevant training in Korea? What?
4. Has she had any relevant training in the United States? What?
5. How much relevant training has Ellen had?

<u>What Do You Think?</u>

1. If the interviewer says to Ellen, "I see you don't have any experience as a typist," what should Ellen say?
2. In your own country, are there special schools you can go to after high school to get job training?

Tasks

A. Read about the applicant. Check the relevant classes and write what to say in the interview. Follow the model.

1. Susan Fong is applying for a job as a receptionist.

    ☐ **a.** first aid/one semester/high school   *I took a switchboard-*

    ☑ **b.** switchboard operating/six weeks/business school   *operating class for six*

                                                weeks in business school.

    ☐ **c.** sewing/two semesters/adult school

2. Dan Cohn is applying for a job as a plumber's apprentice.

☐ **a.** welding/three months/high school _____

☐ **b.** TV repair/one year/adult school _____

☐ **c.** Spanish/two semesters/college _____

3. Carmen Perales is applying for a job as a drafter.

☐ **a.** modeling/four months/modeling school _____

☐ **b.** typing/six months/high school _____

☐ **c.** drafting/three semesters/college _____

4. Sun-wing Lee is applying for a job as a billing clerk.

☐ **a.** driving/five weeks/driving school _____

☐ **b.** French/three months/high school _____

☐ **c.** bookkeeping/two semesters/business school _____

B. Listen to the tape. Listen for information about the applicants' work experience and training. Check the items the applicants described and write the information. Then tell which applicant gave a more complete answer. Follow the model.

JOB	EXPERIENCE	TRAINING

1. accounting

Applicant A

☑ job: *accounting*   ☐ class: _____

☑ length: *a lot*   ☐ length: _____

Applicant B

☑ job: *accounting*   ☑ class: *accounting*

☑ length: *two years*   ☑ length: *eight months*

JOB	EXPERIENCE	TRAINING

2. sales clerk

Applicant A

☐ job: _____ ☐ class: _____

☐ length: _____ ☐ length: _____

Applicant B

☐ job: _____ ☐ class: _____

☐ length: _____ ☐ length: _____

3. plumber's apprentice

Applicant A

☐ job: _____ ☐ class: _____

☐ length: _____ ☐ length: _____

Applicant B

☐ job: _____ ☐ class: _____

_____

☐ length: _____ ☐ length: _____

4. telephone operator

Applicant A

☐ job: _____ ☐ class: _____

_____ _____

☐ length: _____ ☐ length: _____

Applicant B

☐ job: _____ ☐ class: _____

☐ length: _____ ☐ length: _____

On Your Own

What kind of work would you like to do? _____

Complete the chart below with classes relevant to the job you would like to have.

HIGH SCHOOL	COLLEGE	OTHER (ADULT SCHOOL, BUSINESS SCHOOL, . . .)

Do you have any relevant training? _____ What? _____

_____

_____

_____

Lesson Thirty-Three/33 Review

Check Your Listening

A. Read the questions about the conversation. Listen to the conversation. What did the speakers say? Circle the correct answer.

1. Is Mrs. Lee applying for a job as a cashier?   yes   no
2. Does Mrs. Lee have two years of experience?   yes   no
3. Has Mrs. Lee done billing?   yes   no
4. Has Mrs. Lee had any inventory experience?   yes   no
5. Has Mrs. Lee had training in computers?   yes   no
6. Does Mrs. Lee mind if the interviewer calls her supervisor?   yes   no
7. Is Mrs. Lee the last applicant?   yes   no

B. Read the questions about the conversation. Listen to the conversation again. What did the speaker say? Circle the letter of the correct answer.

1. Mrs. Lee is applying for a job as:

   a. an accountant   b. an accountant's assistant   c. an accounting clerk

2. What kind of work has Mrs. Lee done?

   a. She has done billing and prepared inventory.

   b. She has done billing and filed bank reports.

   c. She has prepared payroll and typed checks.

3. The company would prefer someone who can prepare

   a. tax reports   b. bank reports   c. inventory reports

4. Mrs. Lee used to help out in her uncle's

   a. grocery store   b. souvenir shop   c. real estate office

5. Mrs. Lee took computer classes in

   a. adult school   b. junior college   c. business school

6. The interviewer is going to

   a. hire Mrs. Lee   b. call Mrs. Lee   c. interview a few more applicants

Conversation Review

Find a partner and practice the conversation. When there are blanks, use information about yourselves.

Interviewer: What can we do for you today?

Applicant: I'm interested in the position as a _____.

Interviewer: I see. Can you tell me about your experience?

Applicant: I have been a _____.

I have _____.

Interviewer: We prefer someone who has _____.

Applicant: _____.

Interviewer: Good. Have you had any experience in _____?

Applicant: _____.

Interviewer: I'd like to check your references. Do you mind if I call your supervisor?

Applicant: _____.

Interviewer: Well, I have to interview a few more applicants. Thank you for coming.

Applicant: Thank you, _____. Good-by.

Check Your Vocabulary

Read the sentence, look at the picture, and then fill in the blank.

 **1.** I have had experience in

_____ .

 2. When he was a drafter, he

_____ .

 **3.** She built

_____

from 1977–79.

 **4.** She made

_____

in 1979.

 **5.** He helped out in his uncle's

_____ shop
for two years.

6. Mr. Lee has been taking

_____ classes
for six months.

 **7.** Mrs. Garcia has just completed a

_____ class.

8. When she was an electrician, she

installed _____ .

Check Your Grammar

First read the sentences and then fill in the blanks. Follow the models.

A. 1. Did you install thermostats?

Yes, I _installed_ thermostats.

2. Did you draw plans?

No, I _____ plans.

3. Did he repair dishwashers?

Yes, he _____ dishwashers.

4. Did they sew jackets?

Yes, they _____ jackets.

5. Did she do alterations?

Yes, she _____ alterations.

6. Did she drive a truck?

No, she _____ a truck.

B. 1. Have you had any experience handling money?

Yes, I _have handled_ money.

2. Have you had any experience giving injections?

Yes, I _____ injections.

3. Has Joe had any experience replacing springs?

Yes, he _____ springs.

4. Has Rita had any experience sewing shirts?
Yes, she _____ shirts.

5. Have you had any experience making suits?

Yes, I _____ suits.

C. 1. In 1978 he _____ a first-aid class.

   2. Since 1978 he _____ three first-aid classes.

   3. The secretary _____ six letters since 2:30 p.m.

   4. Yesterday the secretary _____ only one letter.

   5. Mr. Chan _____ a taxi from 1972 to 1974.

   6. I _____ shirts five years ago.

D. 1. She _____ an electrician for the past six years.

   2. He _____ an accounting clerk in 1979.

   3. May-ling _____ a cook since 1977.

   4. Jack _____ a typist from 1975 to 1979.

   5. Mr. Vogel _____ a bus driver two years ago in Dallas.

E. 1. She used _____ inventory when she helped out in her father's grocery store.

   2. She also _____ souvenirs.

   3. Mrs. Ito used _____ telephones when she worked in a motel.

   4. They used _____ shelves and cabinets.

   5. They also _____ cabinets.

   6. Peter used _____ records for his father's real estate office.

   7. The editorial assistant used_____ proofreading.

   8. She also _____ copy.

Read and Think

Read the story and then answer the questions.

Before going to an interview, applicants should always plan their answers. They should begin by thinking about their past jobs and looking for relevant experience. For example, someone who is applying for a position as a clerk-typist should look for clerical experience in past jobs. Then in the interview the applicant should talk about the clerical experience.

In interviews, applicants should not just tell the interviewer they have a lot of experience. They should give the name of the job, describe the duties, and tell the employer how long they have been on the job.

Experience does not mean only paid experience. Some people often work without pay for their families or relatives. They should always talk about this kind of experience if it is relevant.

Besides experience, an interviewer would also like to know about relevant training. Therefore, applicants should also talk about classes they have taken in schools if they are relevant. Applicants who can say many good things about themselves have a better chance of getting hired.

Questions

1. What should people do before they go to an interview?
2. When applicants talk about relevant experience, what should they tell the interviewer?
3. Should applicants talk about work that they did for their relatives or families without pay?
4. Besides experience, what else should applicants talk about at an interview?
5. Why should applicants say many good things about themselves?

What Do You Think?

1. When the interviewer asks Mrs. Hill about her work experience, Mrs. Hill answers, "I have a lot of experience." Is that a good answer? Why?
2. Sadat is interviewing for a position as an auto mechanic. He says to the interviewer, "I have taken typing and filing classes in business school." Is that a good answer? Why?
3. Why should applicants talk only about relevant experience?

Put It Together

A. Listen to the interviews. Did the applicants talk about the things on the list? Circle the correct answer.

	Sue	Lily
1. relevant job(s)	yes no	yes no
2. the length of the job(s)	yes no	yes no
3. relevant duties	yes no	yes no
4. relevant training	yes no	yes no

Now tell which applicant you would hire and why.

B. Think of a job you would like. Find a help wanted ad for that job. Put it in the box.

1. Find a classmate or a teacher to interview you. Have that person ask you these questions:

    a. What kind of experience have you had?

    b. Have you had any experience in ___*(required experience in ad)*___ ?

2. Ask your classmate or teacher to listen to your answers and check the items below.

    a. relevant job(s)?   yes   no

    b. the length of your job(s)?   yes   no

    c. relevant duties?   yes   no

    d. relevant training?   yes   no

Vocabulary

A/a

abbreviations (p. 129, L. 23)
ability (p. 140, L. 25)
above (p. 4, L. 1)
abrasion (p. 92, L. 16)
accident (p. 100, L. 18)
accurate (p. 144, L. 26)
acid (p. 90, L. 16)
ad (p. 122, L. 22)
advice (p. 20, L. 4)
airport (p. 59, L. 10)
aisle (p. 101, L. 18)
alkali (p. 92, L. 16)
alterations (p. 172, L. 30)
always (p. 100, L. 18)
And you? (p. 2, L. 1)
anyway (p. 134, L. 24)
apply (p. 122, L. 22)
apprentice (p. 166, L. 29)
Are you? (p. 2, L. 1)
Are you working now? (p. 2, L. 1)
around (p. 54, L. 10)
arrival (p. 48, L. 9)
arrive (p. 48, L. 9)
asbestos (p. 90, L. 16)
assistant (p. 167, L. 29)
at the beginning (p. 125, L. 22)
at the end (p. 125, L. 22)

B/b

back (p. 20, L. 4)
bakery counter girl (p. 137, L. 24)
bank teller (p. 186, L. 32)
banking (p. 186, L. 32)
banking experience (p. 136, L. 24)
bartender (p. 12, L. 2)
because (p. 20, L. 4)
before (p. 8, L. 2)
begin (p. 6, L. 1)
better (p. 26, L. 5)

better chance (p. 155, L. 27)
big (p. 31, L. 6)
bilingual (p. 144, L. 26)
billing (p. 154, L. 27)
bleach (p. 110, L. 20)
blister (p. 91, L. 16)
blow torch (p. 15, L. 3)
blueprint (p. 138, L. 25)
boring (p. 26, L. 5)
boss (p. 85, L. 15)
bracelet (p. 95, L. 17)
breaking a rule (p. 100, L. 18)
breathe (p. 112, L. 20)
build (built) (p. 172, L. 30)
bumpy (p. 55, L. 10)
burn (p. 110, L. 20)
But I learn fast (p. 8, L. 2)
But it is! (p. 55, L. 10)
butcher (p. 15, L. 3)
by bus (p. 43, L. 8)
by ferry (p. 43, L. 8)
by plane (p. 43, L. 8)
by streetcar (p. 43, L. 8)
by subway (p. 43, L. 8)
by train (p. 43, L. 8)
by 6:30 (p. 49, L. 9)

C/c

cab (p. 153, L. 27)
careful (p. 94, L. 17)
carpentry experience (p. 134, L. 24)
carton (p. 100, L. 17)
catch fire (p. 110, L. 20)
category (p. 23, L. 4)
cause (p. 100, L. 18)
chart (p. 191, L. 32)
cheap (p. 43, L. 8)
chemical (p. 85, L. 15)
choose (p. 75, L. 13)
chronological order (p. 4, L. 1)
clean (p. 30, L. 6)
clear (p. 101, L. 18)
climb (p. 104, L. 19)
close (p. 30, L. 6)
comfortable (p. 61, L. 11)
complicated (p. 62, L. 11)
computer (p. 186, L. 32)
computer operations (p. 186, L. 32)

consonant (p. 130, L. 23)
construction (p. 185, L. 32)
convenient (p. 61, L. 11)
copy (p. 173, L. 30)
cord (p. 100, L. 18)
corrosive (p. 110, L. 20)
cost (p. 43, L. 8)
cotton (p. 90, L. 16)
covered can (p. 101, L. 18)
crate vegetables (p. 9, L. 2)
currently (p. 166, L. 29)
cut (p. 91, L. 16)
cutter (p. 139, L. 25)

D/d

dancer (p. 154, L. 27)
dangerous (p. 26, L. 5)
dates employed (p. 5, L. 1)
dental assistant (p. 136, L. 24)
departure (p. 49, L. 9)
describe (p. 19, L. 3)
desired (p. 142, L. 25)
difference (p. 54, L. 10)
difficult (p. 27, L. 5)
direct (p. 74, L. 13)
dirty (p. 30, L. 6)
dishwasher (p. 166, L. 29)
Do you have a minute? (p. 20, L. 4)
Do you mind if I . . . ? (p. 185, L. 32)
Don't give up (p. 144, L. 26)
downtown (p. 45, L. 10)
drafter (p. 167, L. 29)
draw (p. 167, L. 29)
drawer (p. 100, L. 18)
duplicate (p. 9, L. 2)
duplicating fluid (p. 111, L. 20)
duplicating machine (p. 94, L. 20)
during (p. 68, L. 12)

Acknowledgments

PHOTOS: Mexican Workers/United Nations 88; Men Working Coating Pans/Abbott Laboratories 109
Cover/Cameramann International
SAFETY POSTERS: 1–3, 87; 4–6, 88; 1–3, 103/Courtesy of National Safety Council